ANCIENT
ISRAELITE
RELIGION

Ancient
Israelite
Religion

SUSAN
NIDITCH

New York   Oxford

OXFORD UNIVERSITY PRESS

Oxford University Press

Oxford   New York
Athens   Auckland   Bangkok   Bogotá   Bombay
Buenos Aires   Calcutta   Cape Town   Dar es Salaam
Delhi   Florence   Hong Kong   Istanbul   Karachi
Kuala Lumpur   Madras   Madrid   Melbourne
Mexico City   Nairobi   Paris   Singapore
Taipei   Tokyo   Toronto   Warsaw

and associated companies in
Berlin   Ibadan

Copyright © 1997 by Susan Niditch

First published in 1997 by Oxford University Press, Inc.
198 Madison Avenue, New York, New York 10016

First issued as an Oxford University Press paperback, 1998.

Oxford is a registered trademark of Oxford University Press, Inc.

Library of Congress Cataloging-in-Publication Data
Niditch, Susan.
Ancient Israelite religion /
Susan Niditch.
p.   cm.
Includes bibliographical references and index.
ISBN 0-19-509127-2 (cloth).—ISBN 0-19-509128-0 (paper)
1. Bible. O.T.—Theology.   2. Judaism—History—To 70 A.D.
I. Title.
BS1192.5.N53   1997
296' .09'01—dc20   96-31593

7 9 8 6

Printed in the United States of America
on acid-free paper

CONTENTS

ANCIENT
ISRAELITE
RELIGION

1

Religion and the
Ancient Israelites

As you read the phrase "religion of ancient Israel," what do you think of? The phrase has two equally challenging components: the meaning of religion and the identity of the ancient Israelites. I frequently ask new students in my introductory courses to attempt to define religion on the basis of their own experience and expectations. Their efforts can usually be classified under two headings: the social-communitarian level and the personal-individual level. Some think first of shared stories and history, a set of shared values and beliefs that offer advice on how to lead the good and worthwhile life, a set of explanations for the way the world works. They think of communal ceremonies and songs, of rituals that bond, and of institutions. Others think of the spiritual development of the self, of a person's special connection with a suprahuman being, of individual petitions and personal faith, of temptation and conscience.

In fact, religion involves all of the above. Ninian Smart, a scholar

of comparative religions, suggests we study religion and secular ideologies under the broad heading "worldview," a term that refers to an
individual or group's "orientation to life." Questions asked under that
heading grapple with understanding the very nature of existence, our
place in the cosmos, our connections with other human beings, including those within our family and culture as well as those we consider foreign and different. "Worldview analysis" seeks to understand
the symbolic patterns that serve as templates for the patterns of our
existence, the contradictions and tensions in life as well as potential
resolutions, the chaos that threatens and the order we seek. Such symbolic patterns are acted out in ritual performance, retold in ancient-
seeming tales, or encapsulated in proverbs or parables. Why must
human beings suffer? Why must we die? Does another sort of existence follow death or is it simply the end? Does a force (or multiple
forces) control the workings of the universe? If so, can we control
such forces or influence them?

Worldviews—set in traditions, times, places, and cultures—
provide answers to some of the difficult and profound questions
we pose as humans, and the religion of the ancient Israelites, like
those of Hindus, Christians, or modern Jews, dealt with these questions.

Smart also reminds us that worldviews are neither monolithic nor
static (1983:22–31). A group may face differing problems over time
or come to perceive reality differently. Rituals may grow in various
ways; systems of symbols evolve. The earliest Israelites, for example,
had no king, whereas by the tenth century B.C.E. the monarchy developed. One would expect such a change in social structure to relate
to changes or alternate options in worldview. Similarly, there will be
variations in worldview among those who understand themselves to
be part of the same religious traditions. Smart notes, for example, that
a Roman Catholic living in a remote, rural Italian village may express
and perceive his or her Catholicism differently from a Roman busi-
nessperson, yet if asked both would identify themselves as Catholic
and be able to share a fundamental set of beliefs (1983:22–27). So
Yahwists represented in the Hebrew Bible and those not represented

exemplified a spectrum of ancient Israelite religion: the farmer of a highland Judean village and an aristocratic woman from Jerusalem in the ninth century B.C.E. may have viewed God somewhat differently though both were Yahwists. Thus, our challenge in exploring Israelite worldview is not only to search for underlying aspects but also to be attentive to changes and variations.

Smart breaks down the rubric "worldview" into several useful "dimensions." Variants of some of Smart's categories will prove useful in exploring ancient Israel. None of these are self-contained, nor are all of Smart's categories useful to the Israelite case, but they do provide some helpful heuristic headings under which to explore the religion of ancient Israel.

The dimensions proposed by Smart that have been adapted for this study are as follows: the experiential; the mythical; the ritual; and the ethical. The experiential dimension has to do with direct experiences of the numinous—visions, trances, messages from God, and more subtle indications of a divine presence. Is the deity believed to communicate with humans in a visceral fashion so that one who receives a divinely sent message or experiences God's presence sees certain things and feels certain ways? Can one, in some sense, be filled with a supramundane spirit or be transported to a metahuman realm or condition?

The mythic dimension refers to the rich and varied narrative traditions that capture and encapsulate a group's values and beliefs, their fear of chaos and their hope for order, their notions of the ways in which the world truly works. Do certain narrative motifs and patterns recur in a group's traditions? What sets of symbols emerge from these mythic patterns with what significance? Such essential story can be examined on various levels: as universal expressions of the challenges of being human; as culture-bound expressions of a particular group's shared response to these challenges; and as individual authors' versions of such responses.

The ritual dimension of a religious tradition expresses some of the same sets of symbols found in a group's myth, only in dramatic form. Patterns of ritual action help to establish or reestablish a community's sense of the social and cosmic order, resolve tensions that have arisen, and mediate between the flawed realm of humankind and the consummate perfection of God's realm.

The ethical dimension refers to a group's "moral action guides" (Little and Twiss: 28–46). What is perceived by a community to be appropriate treatment of one's fellows? How is one to relate to outsiders? What are the boundaries of proper behavior? Smart also describes a social dimension, referring to the ways in which a group's social structure or mode of interaction as a community reflects and helps shape its worldview. Who is allowed or expected to marry whom? What are key kinship relationships in a society? What is its mode of governance, that is the hierarchies that govern social relations? Interest in the social dimensions of Israelite worldview figures prominently in each chapter of this book as we seek to match the artifacts of Israelite culture, both material and literary, with the people themselves, set in relationships and societies.

In a contemporary tradition, exploring the experiential dimension would involve asking members of a community about their immediate and direct experience of the otherworldly or numinous, the power of the divine or sacred. In working with the ancient, edited, and set writings of the Hebrew Bible, the texts may be reports of such experiences or creative compositions reflecting what their authors thought such experiences should be like. All such reports will be presented in the traditional style of the Hebrew Bible, in which, as in any orally based, traditional culture, there are established ways to describe certain events and experiences, conventions governing image and language that describe a deity's appearances, the devotee's response, and so on. Thus, the experiential is the mythological, for the Hebrew Scriptures are, on a very basic level, value-laden and symbolic narration in which essential aspects of worldview are crystallized.

Similarly, while archaeological finds provide information about altars and instruments, sacred spaces and statuary, fuller descriptions of ritual accoutrements and settings, ritual activities, priestly roles, and the goals of ritual action are set within the larger biblical story in the form of written descriptions now preserved in the various genres that constitute the Hebrew Bible. Legal corpora and prophetic utterances that reveal the ethical dimensions of Israel's worldview are also encorporated into the biblical story. As in the case of ritual, some archaeological information can be of help in exploring social structure. For example, scholars try to reconstruct pictures of the physical setup of villages or cities in order to learn about social stratification. Nevertheless, in the case of the social dimension, as in the others, the Hebrew Bible preserves Israelites'—at least certain Israelites'—views of kinship and other features of social structure and not necessarily facts of social history. Thus, the social dimension also falls within the mythic dimension.

The categories overlap and break down in many other ways as well. Ritual action often reflects and reinforces social structure; ethical lapses may be absolved through ritual action. The moral-action guides urged by some toward those regarded as true members of the group may differ from attitudes toward nonmembers or toward those whom the writers do not regard as true members. Nevertheless, as heuristic categories the dimensions are helpful and provide a way of getting at the tradition.

The Story

The Hebrew Bible weaves a tale. The world is created, ordered, and peopled by God. Next emerge Israel's earliest ancestors from origins in the Fertile Crescent, migrating to a promised land upon orders from Yahweh, their God. In Israel Abraham and Sarah parent Isaac who marries his cousin, Rebecca. Her son, Jacob, marries Rachel and Leah, his cousins, as generation follows generation. Pictured as sojourners or alien residents, the patriarchs and their families move with their flocks, establish altars, and sink wells. They are born, marry, vie for supremacy with one another, mature, die, and bury their dead, laying a physical claim to the land.

One of the Bible's many tales of sibling rivalry—this one involving Rachel's son Joseph and his jealous brothers—and a situation of famine, another frequent biblical theme, lead the descendants of Jacob to settle in Egypt. The sons of Jacob father the tribes of Israel, whose number multiplies in accordance with God's covenantal promises of plenty. A fearful and tyrannical Pharaoh eventually enslaves and op-presses the Israelites, but they are liberated through God's miracle acts, plagues and an event at the Red Sea, and are led out of slavery by Moses and Aaron of the priestly tribe of Levi. The Israelites spend forty years wandering in the wilderness, having experienced God's numinous power and receive his law, which they disobey frequently, setting a pattern of sin, punishment, and forgiveness which comes to characterize their relationship with the deity. Finally they enter the promised land and attempt to settle it. At this time the people live politically and worship ritually in decentralized fashion, without a capital, king, or temple. Led by charismatic leaders called judges, whose victories and defeats are often recounted in the bardic style of epic, the Israelites survive encounters with better-armed enemies in the land, Canaanites and Philistines and others who finally prove too strong for the fledgling Israelite state. The people demand a king and with regret God acquiesces. Then come the monarchies; a united king-dom under Saul; then David, his usurper; the rule of David's son, Solomon; and separate northern and southern kingdoms thereafter, following a post-Solomonic schism. Many prophets arise declaring God's approval or disapproval of Israel's rulers and providing an on-going evaluation of the people's faith. The court histories of the kings, especially David, are filled with intrigue, murder, adultery, incest, and rebellion, although David and his dynasty, which lasts for hundreds of years, are recalled idyllically, David himself becoming ancestor-hero of a hoped-for messiah.

Finally the kingdoms are conquered, the North by the superpower Assyria, the Southern Davidic kingdom by Babylonia, events regarded as punishment for Israel's sin. The temple has been destroyed and the elite of Jerusalem exiled in the so-called Babylonian exile, but they are permitted a safe return to the land by Cyrus some seventy years later, and some do return to rebuild the temple. New prophets arise such as Haggai and Zechariah declaring God's forgiveness and support for the restoration predicted by their predecessors, Jeremiah, Ezekiel, and Deutero-Isaiah. With non-monarchic leaders such as Ezra and Nehe-miah a small Judean polity reemerges under the political control of Persia.

The Bible, Literature, and Social History

This summary account of Scripture's story, of course, leaves out lots of details—indeed, whole biblical books—and all the interesting tensions in style, content, and message that give the tradition its life and make it such fun to study. Nevertheless, the Bible is threaded together by recurring patterns in language and content and is so purposefully historiographic in orientation that it seduces us into taking it on its own terms, into accepting its essential outline of Israelite history and its claims for connections between the rich writings and the lives of actual Israelites set in time and place. Although modern scholarship approaches the Bible's claims to historical and sociological verisimilitude with suspicion, it nevertheless realizes that there are links between the social worlds of the creators of the literature, the participants in the tradition, and the writings in many genres that are now enclosed in the volume called the Hebrew Bible.

The Story Without the Bible

There is, however, a way to explore the Israelite story without using the Hebrew Bible. The resources are sketchier, more varied, and disparate; and they lack the grandiose, orderly wholeness of the biblical tradition, now set between covers and readable from page to page. These resources include archaeological data. For example, archaeological explorations reveal what sort of buildings the Israelites built, lived in, and when; what towns and cities looked like; and the nature of Israel's material culture and agricultural products in various periods and places. Resources also include epigraphic materials, ancient writings on the victory steles of foreign rulers or in the royal correspondence of one of the great ancient Near Eastern empires, the letters written in ink on potsherds found in many locations in the archaeological remains of ancient Israel, and Israelite inscriptions of various kinds. If we rely on such resources, the story goes something like the following:

The Pre-Monarchic Period

By the thirteenth century B.C.E. a group called Israel—so the Egyptian victory stele of Merneptah refers to them—lived in the small piece of land between the Mediterranean and the Arabian Desert. The Mesopotamian city states that spawned great empires were between the Tigris and the Euphrates to the east, Asia Minor to the north, Egypt and Africa to the southwest, and Europe to the northwest. Israelites did not occupy a nation-state that reflects the current borders of modern Israel, nor did they neatly control the entity described variously in the Hebrew Bible as the territory of the twelve tribes, the empire of Solomon, or the gift given to the people by their god, Yahweh. The Israelites were a more decentralized yet identifiable people related in language and culture to the other Canaanite groups around them, living in the central frontier highlands in locations such as Ai, Bethel, Shiloh, and Raddana, all sites that archaeologists have explored. In the view of Finkelstein and others, initial settlement occurred in Ephraim and Manasseh, and "to some degree in Benjamin and Judah. From this core area the new population expanded southward to the Judean hill country and northward to the Galilee" (81).

The Israelites were pastoral people rearing domesticated animals such as cows, sheep, and goats, and agricultural, raising crops such as olives, grapes, dates, figs, pomegranates, cereals, and legumes. They deforested the hills containing all manner of lions and other wild beasts and grew food on terraced plots below their hilltop villages. Soil quality and climate could vary significantly in the highlands, requiring farmers to stagger their crops seasonally and to trade foodstuffs with neighbors from villages in nearby but different eco-niches in order to obtain a wider range of foods (Meyers forthcoming A). Israelite farmers no doubt worried about rain and crops, concerns that dominate so much of the biblical corpus, reminding us not only of Israel's roots but of major continuing themes in Israelite thought.

The highland farmers stored water in bell-shaped cisterns dug into bedrock and sometimes lined with plaster (Stager 1985:4, 9–10). Archaeologists have uncovered silos and storage pits in which Israelites stored grain, as well as the unpainted, collared-rim jars also used for

Figure 1. Four-room house at ʿIzbet Ṣarṭah. (*Courtesy of Professor Israel Finkelstein, Tel Aviv University.*)

food storage. Their villages were small and kin-based (17–20). Remains of homes have been excavated and found to be in cluster arrangements, each small home typically being around fifty feet long and thirty feet wide, consisting of a central room lined with pillars. A space for animals (e.g., the proverbial fatted calf) was located behind each of the pillar lines, while central spaces could be used for cooking and weaving or other cottage crafts, though cooking may have also taken place in protected areas outside the house where smoke could more easily escape (Meyers forthcoming A). At the rear of the pillared house was a small "broadroom" or pantry used for storage. The house served a wide range of economic activities in the interest of household self-sufficiency (Meyers forthcoming A; Holladay 1992:312, 316). Additional rooms upstairs could be built atop the pillars and used for sleeping or living space. This house style not only characterizes the pre-monarchic period but the monarchy as well (Stager 1989:61; 1985: 11–23).

In many ways we imagine the pre-monarchic period to be charac-

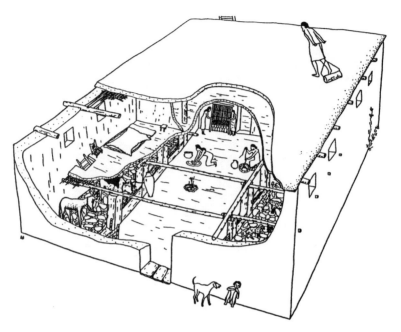

Figure 2. Model of a four-room house as reconstructed by Lawrence E. Stager and drawn by Abbas Alizadeh. (*Courtesy of Professor Lawrence Stager, Harvard University.*)

terized by a pre-state or non-state society without a centralized government, urbanization, or the use of the technology of writing for communication across distances. This technology would become particularly helpful for a centralized military and for the development of commercial activity. Nevertheless, certain chieftains no doubt arose and some villages unified for mutual defense as experiments in statehood took place among early Israelites. Models for states throughout the Near East in the second half of the second millennium B.C.E. would have been plentiful and familiar—if distasteful in many ways—to these frontier pioneers of the highlands.

Traders would have plied the region, even allowing for the highland settlers' relative self-sufficiency. The settlers no doubt included farmers, former mercenaries, merchants, and nomads dislocated as a result of the economic contractions of the Late Bronze Age, all of whom might have contributed to the cultural heritage of the highland Israelites.

What stories would they have told and what worldview did their religious ceremonies express? Were they already familiar with a story of Eden? Did some claim descent from Abraham, Isaac, and Jacob and believe that the land was promised to them by the deity Yahweh? Did the Exodus tradition belong to their founding myths? Does the fact that the Egyptians called these inhabitants of Canaan "Israel" imply the existence of the folk etymology for Jacob's name found in Genesis and the accompanying mythology, or did the etymology and the myth arise later in Israel's history? Did some of the genealogical traditions and stories begin with these Israelites or did they already seem very ancient to them, making true what was the work of the imagination and describing what must have seemed to have always been? Archaeology and extrabiblical sources cannot answer these questions.

And what is one to make of the intriguing circle of stones, with a large stone set on its narrow, long side at the circle's eastern rim, or of the eighteen-centimeter-long bronze statuette of a bull found in the Samarian hills "in the heart of the Israelite settlement region"? (Mazar 1992:350–51). Do these tell us something of ancient Israelite religion in the era before the monarchy? These are questions to ponder as we explore the Hebrew Scriptures, but I believe that the traditions of these early Israelites are somehow incorporated into the multilayered masterpiece which is the Bible.

Life in the frontier would have been difficult, plagued by drought, mudslides on the terraces, competition from other settlers, and roving bandits. This form of subsistence agriculture does tend to make for a high level of interaction and cooperation between the genders. Carol Meyers suggests that women enjoyed a degree of respect and political and economic parity on the frontier and in daily village life that would continue throughout Israel's history, a condition of interdependence and parity that was possibly lost in the urban centers of the monarchy (forthcoming B). One wonders, of course, if an equal share in the backbreaking work of subsistence farming is something to be ideal-

Figure 3. Bronze bull figurine (length 18 cm). (*Courtesy of the Israel Museum, Jerusalem, and the Israel Antiquities Authority.*)

ized. In any event, portrayals of women and implicit attitudes toward women in ancient Israelite literature is one of the paths I hope to explore.

By the mid-tenth century B.C.E. Israelites had made the transition from a society of kinship-based groups living in "widely distributed" hamlets and unfortified villages in the highlands and upper Galilee (Holladay 1994:50)—probably led by councils of elders (Holladay 1994:17) and perhaps eventually by chieftains, who held sway over a somewhat larger group of clans or villages—to a young state, at first still resembling a chieftainship, whose people now controlled the low-lands as well.

The Monarchies

The archaeological record for the tenth century B.C.E. and later (during the so-called Iron Age) reveals a new urban culture, the emergence of

Figure 4. Ashlar masonry at the "high place," Dan. (*Courtesy of Professor A. Biran, Tel Dan Excavations, HUC, Jerusalem.*)

"monumental architecture," with its skill-intensive ashlar, hewn-block masonry, and stone moldings (Mazar 1992:382). Massive fortifications, casement-wall systems, six-chambered gateways, and palace complexes are typical of Iron Age cities in northern and southern kingdoms established in the monarchic period. Each kingdom had its capital, Samaria and Jerusalem, respectively. The latter was a veritable "metropolis," according to the archaeologist Amihai Mazar (424), "a huge city in the eighth and seventh centuries spreading over some 150 acres" (416–17), while Samaria at the time of the northern king Ahab had a magnificent royal acropolis as large as a whole country town (406). Beyond the capitals lay various regional administrative centers such as Hazor, Megiddo, and Lachish. City streets would be made of

Figure 5. Six-chamber gate at Gezer. (*Photograph by Robert B. Wright. Courtesy of Professor William G. Dever, University of Arizona.*)

beaten earth or cobblestones. The infrastructure included stone-lined drainage canals built along the streets and connected to a main drain leading out of the town (470–71). Mazar has us picture some streets opening onto piazzas usually located inside the city gate, while others are alleys with dead ends. Along main streets the front rooms of houses may have formed rows of shops and workshops (470–71). Some cities had quite sophisticated water projects (484), such as Hezekiah's tunnel which brought water into Jerusalem.

On the one hand, the monarchy, with its attendant process of urbanization and varieties of political and economic centralization, could have an impact upon the average Israelite and his or her worldview. The work scene now included careers in the military, with its horse-drawn chariots, or the court bureaucracy, with its scribes and officials; artisans and traders would cater to the tastes and demands of a growing elite, who loved fine wrought ivory, their food seasoned with the spices of India, made available through the Arabian trade route.

The ambitious building projects just described would require the work of trained personnel and perhaps the use of slave labor (Meyers forthcoming B), while funding for palaces, water systems, and massive fortifications might have been provided through the levying of taxes and tolls for traders desiring access through the land (Holladay 1994:29). The great temple of Jerusalem would have been a virtual city within a city, while outlying shrines and sanctuaries such as those at Arad and other smaller towns and cities might have continued to employ, or newly employ, a number of people (Mazar 1992:496; on Lachish during united monarchy, see 499; Holladay 1994: 61).

And yet, as John Holladay and others have pointed out, village life in the agricultural and pastoral modes continued to flourish throughout Israel's history. While some modern scholars, like the writers of the Hebrew Bible themselves, insist that urbanization and the existence of centralized governments led to increasing class stratification, specialization in cash crops, and a new feudalism of estates, Holladay notes that much of the archaeological evidence continues to reveal houses of similar size and structure implying continuity with the lifestyle of the pre-monarchic period (1994: 56–59).

Caution may be in order, in fact, in using terms such as *urbanization* and *city* in connection with these developments during the monarchic period. Certainly cities such as Jerusalem were impressive, but the vast majority of people continued to live in villages, making their living through agriculture even once the monarchy was firmly established (Meyers forthcoming B:). The number of large urban centers with their fortifications and gates was actually quite small. The Hebrew Bible uses the term *city* rather loosely to refer to what were really larger villages. Moreover, as Carol Meyers notes, kinship ties based in village life and the bonds of kinship groups to ancestral lands must have remained important in the sociology of ancient Israel, even with the arrival of the monarchy (forthcoming B).

Scholars note that the eighth and seventh centuries B.C.E. reveal an increased use of the technology of writing. Hundreds of ostraca—writing, usually in ink, on flat pieces of broken clay pots (sherds)—have been found in northern and southern kingdoms, frequently in what seem to have been administrative centers (on Lachish, see Mazar

1992:435; on Arad, see Mazar 1992:440). Some make sweeping claims for Israelite literacy. One scholar points even earlier in the tenth century B.C.E. to a "Solomonic enlightenment" (von Rad 1953:440). And yet these examples of ancient literacy are primarily confined to certain areas: the lively commercial realm, for example, writing on weights and measures or simple messages on jars indicating place of origin or content or ownership; letters communicating commercial or military information; inscriptions of a monumental, event-marking significance (only a few fragments in Hebrew have remained of royal inscriptions, the finest surviving example of monumental inscription commemorates the completion of Hezekiah's water tunnel and was etched into the wall of the building project itself); and blessings, curses, and dedications endowing writing with the transformative, identity-creating, and magical capacity frequently attributed to literacy by the nonliterate.

The availability of writing could provide the average Israelite with a means of communicating with the bureaucracy, as the famous letter of a corvée worker indicates. He uses the letter, no doubt dictated to a local scribe, who inked it upon a sherd, to complain to a government official that his garment has been taken by one Hoshayahu and not returned, contrary to customary law (Exod. 22:25–26). One certainly would not gainsay the importance of writing for communication across distances within the new society of government and military officials, or in the growing economy. Nevertheless, the vast majority of Israelites were not literate in the modern sense. Israel remained a largely oral world in which professional scribes did much of the writing and in which rich narrative traditions, songs, hymns, proverbs, laws, and customs reveal the styles and presuppositions of oral cultures. In such a society the skill of writing was not a social necessity and the oral tradition was respected and perhaps even preferred for certain activities.

What about the lives of women in the new urban culture? As the pillared houses with their implications about the continued vitality of family-centered units continued, so the traditional roles of women continued in patrilineal and patrilocal households. Meyers points to a continued interdependence between the genders in the village life of the majority of people (Meyers forthcoming B). Holladay suggests that, as in many traditional cultures, there were women's spaces and men's spaces in the cities. The women's locus was perhaps in the market by day but certainly in home areas used for the loom, other cottage crafts, and cooking, while the men's locus is public, for example, by the city gate where the elders meet. Meyers and others suggest that in urban centers like Jerusalem women do become more confined to the private realm, no longer their husbands' political equal, as in the days of subsistence farming on the frontier (Meyers forthcoming B). Scholars have seen similar patterns in the roles of women in the American West or within the early Israeli kibbutzim. Of course, for the relatively few aristocratic women belonging to the royal-related elite, new possibilities may have opened up for personal development and even for leadership roles as queen mothers (Ackerman 1993), royal prophetesses, and so on. Avigad points to the fact that some women had cylinder seals of their own during the monarchy and the subsequent postexilic period (205–6), indicating a certain public position, for the seal lends a document or object one's own personal stamp, indicating ownership or identity and in the process asserts one's status and power. Would you rather be a humble but equal farmer's wife or a somewhat more sequestered female aristocrat, gazing out from latticework windows, waiting on a couch of ivory for the return of your charioteer husband? These are, of course, complex questions in social history.

Various temple sites and accoutrements have been unearthed, dating from the period of the monarchy; for example, horned ashlar altars from sanctuary sites at Dan in the north and Beersheba in the south (Mazar 1992:496). Mazar speculates that these altars were in use in the ninth century B.C.E. (494–95). A small temple has been excavated at Arad of Judah. At the entrance Mazar describes its "holy of holies," a special sacred space, what Mazar interprets to be two stone altars opposite two standing stones that may be symbolic representations of the deities or of their indwelling presence (497; see also McCarter 1987:148–49). An assortment of additional cultic paraphernalia have been found at various sites, such as cult stands and incense bowls, seven-sprouted lamps, and a variety of figurines (see Holladay 1987:

Figure 6. Painting and inscription on a large jar from Kuntillet ʿAjrud. The inscription includes the phrase "Yahweh of Samaria and his asherah." (*Courtesy of Professor Z. Meshel, Tel Aviv University.*)

265–66, 272–73). Hundreds of pottery female figurines have been found in northern and southern kingdoms that Mazar attributes to women's home rituals having to do with fertility (Mazar 1992: 501; cf. Meyers 1988: 161). Equally intriguing from the period of the monarchy, is the site of Kuntillet ʿAjrud, about fifty kilometers south of Kadesh-Barnea. The original building appears to have been rectangular, surrounded on three sides by "long casement rooms" (Mazar 1992:447). Benches were built along the walls, with benches, walls, and floors covered by white plaster. At this site were found dedicatory inscriptions, blessings, and drawings "on wall plaster, on two larger jars, and on a stone vat" (447). The shape of the writing in these inscriptions points to a possible date in the early eighth century B.C.E. One of the drawings depicts five male figures with arms raised (see figure 7). Another shows three figures: two standing, a male, and a female, and one seated figure of indeterminate gender; the seated being has an animal head and appears to play the lyre, while one standing figure perhaps wears a three-horned crown (see figure 6). The standing male figure appears to have a tail, and both standing figures have been described as possessing bovine features. This drawing is accompanied by an inscription that includes the phrase "to Yahweh of Samaria and his Ashera," part of a dedicatory formula found more than once at this site and possibly at other sites as well (see McCarter 1987:143 on Cave II at Khirbet el-Qom). These are, to say the least, intriguing but difficult to interpret pieces of evidence. (See the debate between McCarter and Coogan versus Tigay in Tigay: 172–75, 180.)

Equally interesting is information that can be gleaned from monarchic-period Israelite burial sites, although one needs to realize that preserved sites probably reflect the lives and beliefs of those wealthy enough to maintain tombs for their departed. Judean burial caves, the earliest and simplest examples dating from the ninth century B.C.E., resemble in plan the form of the "four-room" house in which Israelites typically dwelt. The tomb thus becomes home to the deceased. The more elaborate tombs of Jerusalem cemeteries are adorned with architectural detail befitting the status and station of its inhabitants. Israelite burial spaces contain the remains of various offerings; pottery vessels used for food and drink libations are common, as are oil lamps. Tombs sometimes contain the seal of the deceased, "together with various weapons, jewelry and other objects" (Mazar 1992:521–26). Some caves include inscriptions, curses to ward off intruders or blessings. Particularly good examples of the latter come from a burial tomb at Ketef Hinnom, small silver plaques engraved with versions of the so-called priestly blessing found in Num. 6:24–25. Were the lamps believed to light the way of the deceased on his journey to the afterlife, as Mazar suggests (525), or did they serve other pragmatic or symbolic functions? Were the offerings meant to satiate the appetite of the dead so that they might quietly lie in peace rather than wander hungry and restless among the living? Were the offerings intended to propitiate the deity who rules over life and death, or are the containers all that remains of a mourner's wake? Does the seal identify the one who is

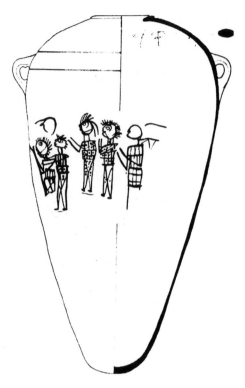

Figure 7. Painting on a large jar at Kuntillet ʿAjrud. (*Courtesy of Professor Z. Meshel, Tel Aviv University.*)

buried, being a symbol of his presence, or is it believed that he needs his things around him as he enters a new and permanent phase in his existence?

The Post-Monarchic Period

The last quarter of the eighth century in the northern kingdom and the first quarter of the sixth in the southern kingdom bring profound changes. The north is conquered by Assyria, its leaders and a portion of its population exiled and replaced with newcomers of different cultures. The former northern kingdom is divided into several Assyrian administrative districts. A decidedly Assyrian style becomes apparent in artifacts and residences. This influence is also found in the South. The great southern city of Lachish had been conquered by Sennacherib in 701 B.C.E., an event commemorated in the Assyrian reliefs now housed in the British Museum, although Judah retained its political independence. By the late sixth century, as the power of the Assyrian empire is eclipsed, the southern kingdom again has some influence over northern life. The southern kingdom of Judah is itself conquered by Babylonia, its elite exiled in 597 and 587–86 B.C.E., and the great temple in Jerusalem destroyed in the second confrontation. Mazar (1992: 548) and Barkcay (1992:372) argue for continuity in material culture despite the conquest, suggesting that the disaster affects "only Jerusalem and the limited territory of late-monarchic Judah," with sites in Gibeon, Mizpah, and Bethel testifying to survival and vitality. The culture as a whole, as archaeological remains reveal, however, is greatly disrupted as major population centers disappear (indicated by burial sites; Holladay, oral presentation, 1994), and the elegant administrative framework set up by the Judean kings crumbles (See the conclusions of Carter 1992:320–21 and Hogland 1992:6–29).

A new frontier, in a sense, opens with the Persian period (late sixth century B.C.E.), when some Israelite exiles return with Persian blessings to Judah and restore life to a now much diminished and no longer independent state (see Hogland 1992:241–47). It is these late Israelites who put their own stamp and ideology on the writings of the Hebrew Bible, though earlier and competing worldviews remain discernable.

One might well ask what this lengthy recounting of history through the eyes of archaeologists and students of extrabiblical sources has to do with the religion of Israel. Clearly, matters such as ecology, climate, house size, means of income, and types of crops are all relevant to issues of worldview, to the way we as human beings make sense of the world around us and understand our place in the cosmos. Such matters are of interest to students of religion. Yet knowing what sort of crops grew in the Judean hills of the first millennium B.C.E. or even finding altars, inscriptions that mention particular deities or Yahweh as variously described and perceived, or discovering statuary such as

Figure 8. Female figurines. (*Courtesy of the Israel Museum and the Israel Antiquities Authority.*)

the small female figurines that many attribute to Israel's religious life will not fully answer fundamental questions about how Israelites dealt with chaos and the various uncontrollable forces of the universe that confront all of us, such as violent weather and other natural disasters, illness, the power of human emotions, even death itself. What did Israelites perceive as governing the forces of life and death? How did they explain the suffering of the good and the prospering of the evil? What orders the cosmos, if anything? What defines "us" versus "them?" What are the relationships between the individual and society, the nuclear family and the larger group, our group and theirs? For ancient Near Easterners the answers to these questions are intimately involved with humans' relationship to a powerful deity or deities.

Artifacts such as the horned altars found at Dan and Beersheba do provide some information. Israelites who lived in the early northern and southern monarchies offered sacrifices on stone altars to otherworldly powers. During the heyday of the monarchy, decorations on religious objects frequently do not depict the deity; thus, some thread in Israelite tradition is aniconic and does not represent the deity anthropomorphically or the like (Holladay 1987:280). Even once the great temple of Solomon exists in Jerusalem, there are outlying shrines in the north and south. Thus, public worship does not appear to have been fully centralized in one place. As for the female figurines, it has been suggested that these are connected to worship of versions of the great ancient Near Eastern goddesses (Mazar 1992:501), though such suggestions are hypothetical (Meyers 1988:161). Certainly some female power is implied. The dedicatory inscription found at Kuntillet 'Ajrud ("to Yahweh of Samaria and his Ashera") and the accompanying drawing may imply that some believed Yahweh had a female consort and that Yahweh was worshiped in a variety of local forms (McCarter 1987:141–42). Burial customs seem to indicate belief in an afterlife and, among many, participation in special ritual activities involving remembrance or propitiation of the dead, such as the offering of libations in the burial tomb.

But all such information is fragmentary and presents no real set of beliefs or worldviews, no real answers to complex questions about Israel's religious tradition. To approach such questions, we need fuller sets of symbols contained in a variety of genres: shared stories that reinforce values and provide a vision of a people's origins and hopes for the future; legal materials by which people perceive themselves to be governed; and descriptions of the deity in action, of the worshiper's devotion. Here we find ourselves turning back to the Hebrew Scriptures.

The Hebrew Bible: Variety and Tradition

The Hebrew Bible is a work of great continuity and constant variety in terms of style, content, and theme. Its compositions include a host of different genres, such as narratives of many types, oracles, songs, sayings, and legal dicta. Of course, Israelites have their own terms and concepts for many of these genres. For example, the *mashal* is a category of literature which can include sayings, parables, and other literary forms that we recognize under other rubrics. Some genres

apparently found their social contexts among specific segments of the
Israelite community, for example, the so-called lawsuit form employed
by prophets to chastise Israel for her lack of faithfulness to God. It is
hypothesized that the juridical language of this form may have had its
origins in actual legal contexts. One would expect the many descriptions of ritual and ritual objects in Exodus, Leviticus, and Numbers
to have been preserved by priests involved in Israelite cultic life.

Biblical compositions that share these various sorts of social context
and origin on some level all belong to a corpus of traditional literature
in which particular literary forms, themes, and linguistic formulas
recur. In the tradition there are ways to describe the birth of a hero,
the meeting of a wife, or to express the way one has experienced an
encounter with the deity. There are recurring phrases that convey
certain messages within individual passages and across the tradition.
These recurring forms exhibit remarkable continuity over time. For
example, the essentials of the symbolic-vision form, one of the media
that describes a prophet's experience of the heavenly realm and the
receiving of divine messages, is found in the eighth-century B.C.E.
work of the prophet Amos, in the seventh and sixth-century work of
Jeremiah and sixth-century Zechariah, and in the second-century
B.C.E. visions of the book of Daniel. The form changes and is developed
to suit new times, contexts, tastes, and thematic needs, but remains
recognizable in its pattern of content and in aspects of its language.
These recurring forms give the Hebrew Bible a certain wholeness and
reflect the oral context that was the world of ancient Israel. This is
not to suggest that every composition of the Hebrew Bible had its
origin in extemporaneous oral performance—though this may well be
true of some works—but rather to suggest that what are now clearly
written works nevertheless reveal the aesthetics and mentality of an
oral world. In such a traditional culture, storytelling, the use of sayings, and other activities represented in the selections now contained
in the Hebrew Bible were regularly carried on without the aid of writing and within literary conventions that serve to repeat and reinforce
aspects of worldview, certain keys to the culture.

Although they share a wide array of literary conventions and the
worldviews implied by such conventions, Israelites were not, however,

a monolithic community over time or at any given time. In addition to the types of spheres of interest concerning priests and prophets mentioned earlier, Israelite society, from the tenth century on, was complex. Changes would occur over time. In the Judean monarchy of the seventh century B.C.E., for example, there would have been rural and urban folk, aristocrats and farmers, rich and poor, old and young, men and women. Some of these differences in identity are no doubt reflected in the range of voices and views now found in the Hebrew Bible and in voices and views that have virtually been edited out of the corpus.

Israelite or Biblical?

The Hebrew Bible itself reveals certain changes and variations over time. The earliest Israelites had no central temple, no king, and no urban center, whereas those in the monarchies did. Israelites who are biblically represented at any one time often disagree on central issues in worldview. For example, not all Israelites wanted a monarchic form of government, worshiped Yahweh alone, or were against iconic representation of the deity. The Bible presents many of these debates overtly, whereas others are presented more implicitly through the polemics that condemn what some Israelites are doing. The Bible does have certain dominant points of view that support particular beliefs and condemn others. These are probably ones which those raised as Jews or Christians will recognize instantly. For example, there is only one god. He is envisioned primarily as male, but rarely or incompletely seen, if at all, by human beings. Human sacrifice is condemned, but animal sacrifice is much appreciated by God. The land, Jerusalem, and the temple are sacred centers for Israel's relationship with Yahweh, God of the ancestors, the Davidic king, a divinely anointed mediator whose reign is in some sense eternal.

This is the point of view of a southern, that is, Judean, Jerusalem-based, pro-Davidic, male-centered group. One might therefore assume that such a group is responsible for the final form of the particular set of Israelite compositions that we call the Hebrew Bible, but they are not representative of all Israelites in the lengthy social history I have described, nor are they responsible for all biblical compositions—even if they did have the final word. To raise these questions already is to suggest that the Bible is a selection from a wider range of materials that were part of Israelite tradition. The final redactors or composers of the Bible worked with an inherited corpus of tradition, but the voices we hear so strongly in the Old Testament may have been those of the minority in a larger culture, only hints of which are preserved in the Hebrew Bible. The crucial questions thus become not only who wrote the Bible but also what the others believed.

Who Wrote the Bible and What Did the Others Believe?

My ancestors would have believed that the Bible in its entirety was dictated by God to Moses on Mount Sinai. Beginning in the seventeenth century and more extensively in the nineteenth century, scholars began to explore the possibility that the Hebrew Scriptures took shape over time through the combining and revision of various sources whose differences in vocabulary, style, content, and theme remain discernable in the current canon. Particular interest was focused on the first five books, the so-called Pentateuch, for which Julius Wellhausen propounded his famous documentary hypothesis (see Knight 1983). Building on the work of others, Wellhausen suggested that the Pentateuch is composed of layers or blocks of material that once existed as independent written documents dating from the period of the monarchy or later. Current versions of his theory set the sources and their dates as follows:

1. The "J" or Jahwist source, said to be found in Genesis–Numbers, usually dated to the tenth-century B.C.E. united monarchy, whose center was Jerusalem of Judah. The name of this document derives from the God-name Yahweh (Jahweh in German) employed by the source. This term is translated as "Lord" in most English Bibles. The deity in this source is said to "walk in the garden," and to speak to humans in a down-to-earth, anthropomorphized fashion.

2. The "E" or Elohist source, in evidence in Genesis–Numbers and often attributed to the ninth-century B.C.E. northern court of the period of the divided monarchy. This source supposedly portrays the

deity in a more transcendent form, employing dream experiences and angels in depicting interactions between the deity and humans. The source is also said to avoid the revelation of God's sacred name until a scene with Moses himself in the book of Exodus. Thus, in Genesis the deity is called the more generic Elohim (the "E" term), translated as "God" in most English Bibles.

3. The priestly source, "P," prominent in Leviticus and Numbers, books that preserve information about ritual, ritual objects and spaces, purities, sacrifice, and other typically priestly concerns. "P" is also regarded as a sixth-century B.C.E. unifying layer in Genesis–Numbers. This source, attributed to Jerusalem priests in Babylonian exile, portrays God as even more transcendent, also avoiding the name Yahweh until Exodus, and is held responsible for many of the genealogical lists in the first four books of the Bible, often framed by the rubric "These are the generations."

4. The seventh-century B.C.E. "D" or Deuteronomic source, responsible for the prevailing outlook of the book of Deuteronomy. "Deuteronomic" writers are also regarded as the shapers of the corpus in Deuteronomy–2 Kings (see Friedman 1987).

For a scholar who accepts these sources, matching up the texts of the Pentateuch with social context and real people thus becomes relatively straightforward. Texts in the "J" source, for example, are tenth-century B.C.E. southern, courtly productions. Of course, many of us find the scheme too neat to be true. Scholars vary widely in their assignment of verses to sources. They debate whether "J" is a school or an individual and whether there even is a separable "E" source (see the classic critique in Nielsen 1961). Other scholars who engage in source criticism for Genesis–2 Kings define and date the sources in radically different ways than Wellhausen's intellectual offspring (see Van Seters 1977, 1983, 1992; Rendtorff 1986).

In contrast to the source critics, some scholars concentrate on the final product that makes for a Pentateuch (Genesis–Deuteronomy) or a Deuteronomic History (Deuteronomy–2 Kings) and suggest that behind such a product, whatever its earlier sources, lie the voice, vision, and worldview of one antiquarian historiographer similar to the Greek Herodotus. In its extreme versions, this theory suggests that the Bible reveals the worldview of this historian and the concerns of his times but provides no information about earlier or other Israelite worldviews. Other scholars leave behind questions of history and literature altogether, exploring instead the meanings and messages that arise between them as contemporary readers and the text. Such scholars emphasize that any reading is subjective and that the responses of past audiences may be irretrievable.

I still believe that it is possible to speculate about the real people behind the literature, the goals of authors, the expectations of audiences, the social context of the compositions, and the worldviews of those who produced, received, transmitted, and preserved the literature. I suggest, however, that one proceed with caution; we are engaged in an exploratory intellectual journey. Old documentary hypotheses or new versions that dice and splice up Scripture into blocks or layers—sometimes even half a line is assigned to one source, and the other half to another—are not convincing to me. How, then, can we match the literature to the real people who have left only fragmentary hints of themselves in the archaeological and literary records, both biblical and epigraphic?

One guideline is provided by style, the most basic issues of vocabulary, orthography, and the way words are used in metric, syllabic, or syntactic combinations. I am convinced, for example, by arguments based on style that Exodus 15, Judges 5, and Deuteronomy 33 are quite ancient Israelite works predating the monarchy, from the twelfth to the eleventh centuries B.C.E. (see Cross and Freedman 1975). Equally convincing are studies that suggest that the variety of Hebrew employed in such late prophets as Zechariah and Haggai offers a guide to the postexilic (sixth century B.C.E. or later) dates of compositions employing a similar style and vocabulary (see Hurwitz 1974). Works in Isaiah 1–39 admit of a different poetic style than works in Isaiah 40–55, which in turn differs in poetic style from chapters 55–66. And yet so much of the Bible's language is in its traditional style rather homogeneous. The writers seek to be part of the tradition and, of course, the case can always be made that a later writer archaizes on purpose. Some scholars, for example, date the book of Ruth to the monarchy, while others date it to the postexilic period. Caution is again recommended.

Equal caution is necessary in matching up archaeological finds with biblically provided information. In the 1950s and 1960s it was axiomatic that thirteenth-century B.C.E. archaeological evidence of burning and destruction in Israelite cities could be matched, at least in general terms, with the biblical portrayal of the conquest. Evidence from Nuzi, Mari, Egypt, and other ancient kingdoms was cited to support the notion that the way of life described for the patriarchs Abraham, Isaac, and Jacob suited and reflected an actual second-millennium B.C.E. setting (see, e.g., Bright 1981). In recent years most scholars have become suspicious of these supposed proofs of the Bible's version of Israel's early history, viewing them as motivated less by objective evaluation of the evidence than by confessionally based desires to prove the Bible to be literally true.

Always we are reminded that the biblical voices are partial, reflecting the point of view of the Bible's authors, sometimes revealing only indirectly the worldviews of many or most Israelites. In recent years scholars have explored a complex of related themes found in the subtexts of the Hebrew Bible and supported by ethnographic models from neighboring cultures and by interpretations of epigraphic and other archaeologically discovered evidence. The themes center on love and death. They concern what the framers of the Hebrew Bible would have considered unorthodox means of procuring fertility in the land and in persons, and with rituals surrounding the propitiation of the dead. The former involve rituals in which human sexuality assures the land's fertility. A sacred marriage is undertaken between a male adherent (or the king himself) and a woman who represents the power of the earth, the feminine, and the fertile. Some scholars suggest that the woman was a special priestess who takes upon herself the role of goddess. Others suggest that female adherents were transformed by the ritual occasion. The love-act was believed to produce fertility and fullness in the land in a sympathetically magical way. The death rituals involve assumptions concerning the capacity of the dead to trouble or assist the living even in their ghostlike existence as shades in Sheol, a place comparable to the classical Greek Hades. Again the notion of propitiating the unquiet dead was unacceptable to the dominant voices of the Bible. An unsavory thread in these themes of love and death involves human sacrifice—especially the sacrifice of children—paradoxically related to issues of fertility (see Heider 1985; J. Day 1989; Lewis 1987, 1989). Indeed, all three aspects of Israelite religious life— fertility rituals, cults of the dead, and human sacrifice—and the stories, scenes, and other snippets of Scripture that suggest their existence in ancient Israel reflect essential beliefs about the cycle of life (see Ackerman 1992). One should add that not all scholars are convinced that all or some of these threads were aspects of Israelite religion.

Finally, it is important to remember that biblical texts are gendered and that the male voice dominates. We would do well, for example, to ask what stories about successful female tricksters may reveal about the audiences and authors of the material and about Israelite worldview. Can we find more in the tradition than men's various attitudes toward women and learn something about women's religious worldviews and the roles of women in Israel's religious life? Was women's religion different from men's religion in some sense? Is there an identifiable women's voice in the literary evidence of the Bible?

In writing about Israelite religion, we seek to understand the synchronic and diachronic dimensions—elements found throughout the life of the tradition and the ways in which they develop over time— and to appreciate the range and diversity within the tradition at any one period. The religion of Israel is characterized by certain fundamental aspects of worldview and certain shared symbols, stories and dramatic reenactments that define what is considered Israelite for nearly one thousand years. There are, however, a number of ways of being Israelite within those parameters, involving changes over time and differences in any single period. The soundings from the Hebrew Bible that follow point to some of the recurring and fundamental ways in which Israelites defined themselves and revealed and preserved their worldview, but they also reflect developments in key concepts over time as well as variations in worldview and the variety of voices behind them.

SUGGESTED READINGS

Good introductory books on the study of religion include Smart's *Worldviews* (1983), and his longer *Religious Experience of Mankind* (1969), Berger's, *Sacred Canopy* (1967), and Geertz's, *Interpretation of Cultures* (1973).

On archaeological approaches to the history and religion of Israel, see in the bibliography to this volume works by Ben-Tor, Dever, Holladay, Mazar, Meyers, and Stager. Also see the various essays in *Biblical Archaeology Today*, edited by Biran. On the postexilic period, see works by Stern, Hogland, and Carter. For studies focusing on the lives of women, see Meyers's *Discovering Eve* (1988).

On the Bible as traditional literature, see Niditch, *Underdogs and Tricksters* (1987), *Folklore and the Hebrew Bible* (1993a), and Niditch, ed., *Text and Tradition* (1990).

Concerning theories about biblical composition: For the classic source–critical approach, see works by Wellhausen and Knight's discussion of Wellhausen. For a modern version of Wellhausen's theories, see Friedman. For modern source-critical treatments of biblical texts, see works by Coote, Coote and Ord, Speiser, and Hyatt. For a classic criticism of source-critical approaches, see Nielsen. Read the story of Noah with Nielsen and see what you think.

While some scholars accept the essential contours of source-critical theory and methodology, they reach conclusions about dating and provenance of the sources quite different from those of Wellhausen, Friedman, Speiser, Coote, and Hyatt. For such approaches, see the works of Rentdorff, Rose, and Van Seters.

Other scholars have taken a more holistic approach to Scripture, setting aside source-critical—and, indeed, historical—questions and asking instead what arises from an encounter between a sensitive modern reader and a text. A recent work by Gunn and Fewell provides an example of such an approach. For an approach that emphasizes wholeness, see Polzin.

For a still influential analysis of Israelite history that relies on more old-fashioned matches between the literature of the Hebrew Bible and archaeological and extrabiblical information, see Bright. For a vehement critique of this approach, see Thompson's recent work.

On threads in Israelite popular religion discussed in this book, see Ackerman. On human sacrifice, see works by J. Day, Heider, Hackett, and Levenson. On cults of the dead, see Bloch-Smith, Lewis, and Schmitt, who differ in their interpretations of the evidence. On the worship of Asherah and other issues in Israelite polytheism, see the works by Smith and Olyan.

To explore the inscriptions mentioned in this chapter and to gain a wider view of extant examples of nonbiblical ancient Isralite writings, see Smelik.

2

The Experiential

To me a word was brought in stealth
and my ear received an inkling from it.
In disquieting thoughts from visions of the night
when the god-sent deep sleep falls upon humans
dread summoned me and trembling.
It filled all my bones with dread.
A spirit swept by my face
and the hair of my flesh bristled.
Something stood but I could not recognize its appearance.
A form was in front of my eyes.
There was silence, then I heard a voice.

Job 4:12

All too often the religion of ancient Israelites is thought of in concrete, of-this-earth terms: a covenant that requires of Israel certain ethical-legal requirements; a God who acts in history; and a ritual life largely based upon sacrifice. Words such as "pragmatic" and "earthy" come to mind at the expense of "spiritual", "inner", and "experiential." In fact, Israelites were acutely and passionately concerned with the experiential dimension, as this brief excerpt from the speech of Eliphaz in Job indicates. The numinous is experienced in a personal, strongly visceral manner, down to the very bones of one's body. It is mysterious, secret, not quite describable yet real and capable of enveloping mere mortals in the process of revelation.

In the biblical Israelite tradition, descriptions of the experiential usually involve encounters with the deity Yahweh himself, who is variously powerful and enigmatic, supportive or threatening. Indeed, the way in which God is perceived and the differing nature of the encounters reveal much shading and variation in Israelite worldview. Experiences of the deity frequently include: the actual appearance of God or his emissary and the indication that he speaks; an interaction; the receiving of a message; the asking and answering of questions; and the human's emotional response of fear, awe, and wonder. Versions of these general motifs appear in the following: scenes in which the human being forges or defines a relationship with God on earth so that God or a symbol of the deity actually appears on earth; in initiation and other visions in which the seer is transported to the heavenly realm; in annunciation scenes in which parents are informed about divine plans for their children or children-to-be; and in aggressive threats to the welfare of the human being by a demonic form of the deity.

Covenant-Making with Men

One of the most fundamental trajectories in the Hebrew Bible deals with the covenantal relationship between God and humans. God promises to a person blessings of land and fertility, offers a sign as confirmation, frequently revealing his own divine identity by a name, and adds to or transforms the experiencer's own identity with a new name or new charge and responsibility. Grounded in legal or political notions of contract, compact, or treaty, the covenant is in Israelite worldview a manifestation of the bond between Israel and God, an expression of mutual obligation mediated by the experience of particular human beings who are enabled to sense, hear, or see the very presence of God.

A simple covenant is found in the story of the good man Noah, sole survivor, with his family, of the flood sent by God to punish a violent and unworthy humanity. God's presence and his promise never to destroy humankind again (Gen. 8:21; by flood 9:11) is conveyed through words by a heard yet unseen deity.

The longer covenant-making scene between Abraham (Abram) and God includes potent and significant visual dimensions (Genesis 15). The word of the Lord comes "in a vision" as the auditory and the visionary mingle on a plane of the suprareal. The word of God promises Abram greatness in progeny and possession of the land and identifies the speaker as Yahweh, the one who had already forged a relationship with Abram in Ur (Genesis 12). The promise is sealed in a ritual scene. Abram prepares an offering specified by the deity, an arrangement of three sacrificial animals cut in half and two whole birds. Then, at sunset, a "deep sleep" falls upon Abram. The trancelike sleep is also said to be experienced by Adam before Eve is formed from his rib (see also Job 4:12 translated above). The term signals the entrance of the sacred into the realm of the mundane. Abram is said to experience "a great terror of darkness," receives prophecy, and then in the dark a smoking pot and a flaming torch pass through the sacrificial pieces. As in the Exodus account and the wider lore of the ancient Near East, the powerful deity is associated with fire. The scene is strongly experiential: the fear, the smoky heat, and the darkness illuminated only by the torch all testify to a writer's view of what it is like to encounter the power of God. A similar pattern of covenant-making is found in Genesis 17—involving motifs of promise, identification of the deity, transformation of and instructions to the human being—but the interaction is verbal and the experiential, as in the Noah tale, is greatly reduced.

On the other hand, Exodus 3, one of the archetypal scenes in the Hebrew Bible concerning a leader's initiation, is rich in the atmosphere of experience. An angel of the Lord appears in a flame of fire from the midst of a bush. The bush blazes but is not consumed by the flame

(3:2). In the covenantal pattern, God reveals his identity to Moses, reiterates his promise of the land, and charges Moses with leading the Israelites out of slavery. In the theophany of Exodus 3, Yahweh strongly identifies himself as Israel's rescuer. He knows of the Israelites' misery and suffering and identifies with their workaday experiences as oppressed slaves. This is the comforting, uplifting message of the experiential. The sensual context for the covenant is charged with the numinous, electric with the fiery heat betokening divine power and the miraculous, as fire burns but does not consume. The author of this account wants us to feel the flame, to hear the voice declaring the space sacred. "Take your sandals off your feet, for the place where you stand is holy ground" (5). The author of this material describes a scene which his audience regards as miraculous but believable. They and we are drawn into the realm of the sacred.

One of the most famous biblical scenes rich in the experiential is found in Exodus 19, the scene at Mount Sinai when Yahweh— warrior god, god of fire, and lawgiver—expresses his power to Moses and the Israelites before revealing the Ten Commandments, stipulations of his covenant with the people of Israel.

The Israelites have been warned to keep their distance from the mountain lest the power of God burst forth upon them (Exod. 19:12; 24). They are to cleanse themselves, the state of ritual purity being necessary to encounter the divinity. They wash their clothes and are ordered not to approach women sexually (19:14–15). Communication here is to men in the public arena.

The entrance into holiness is accompanied by thunder and lightning; a thick cloud covers the mountain and a trumpet blast issues forth so loud that all the people who are in the camp tremble in terror. The smoke is like the smoke of a kiln, Sinai is wrapped in smoke, and the Lord descends upon the mountain in fire. The mountain shakes violently as the trumpet blast grows louder and louder (Exod. 20:16–19). In the midst of this charged situation Moses ascends to meet God (see also 20:18–21). The imagery of the experiential is drawn from the natural realm—some of the most frightful aspects of climate and earth's behavior that we experience—but such occurrences are perceived to be monumental markers of the presence of

God. Comparable fire imagery appears in Moses' experience at Exod.
24:15–18. Such motifs are typological and recur throughout the tradition, yet they are not regarded universally as sure indicators of the
divine presence.

Quite unusual in this respect is the experience of Elijah described
in 1 Kings 19. Depressed by Queen Jezebel's persecutions of Yahwists
such as himself—her devotion is to the god Baal and his priests—
Elijah flees into the wilderness, hoping to die. He falls asleep under a
broom tree and is wakened by the touch of an angel, who provides
him with food. He eats and then lies down again. Again the angel
touches him and urges him to eat. Elijah the holy man experiences
God's bounty miraculously in a visitation of an angel at the temporal
boundary marking the passage from sleep to wakefulness. The capacity
to produce or withhold food is the very essence of God-power, a power
Elijah himself is allowed to manipulate (1 Kings 17:10–16). Elijah
then travels forty days and nights—an evocative biblical number, the
years spent in the wilderness and Moses' days on the mountain (Exod.
24:18)—to "Horeb" (another term for Sinai, the scene of the Sinai
covenant), to a cave. Is this the very site where Moses himself had
been allowed to see God's glory, the back of the deity who is somehow
anthropomorphized? God covers Moses and protects him from the
divine power, for according to Exod. 33:20 "no one can see God's face
and live." In 1 Kings 19 the motifs of storm god theophany reappear,
as would be expected by an audience reading or hearing about Elijah's
experience. A receiver of this story participates in a wider ancient Near
Eastern tradition concerning appearances of the deity, but more specifically Elijah is presented as a second Moses, following in his foot-
steps and undergoing his experiences. Perceptions of the great
charismatic leader of the Exodus tradition shine upon and frame expectations for the holy man Elijah. Remarkably, although there is a
tornado-force wind, Yahweh is not in the wind; there is an earthquake,
but Yahweh is not in the earthquake; there is a fire, but Yahweh is not
in the fire. What concludes the typical theophanic array is a most
atypical thin whisper, literally "a silent, powder-fine voice" (1 Kings
19:12). Elijah hears it and emerges from the cave to hear the words
of God. This is then, a fascinating surprise theophany, perhaps shock-

ing to those in the tradition. The scene in 1 Kings 19 makes a point about the nature of the deity and the quality of God-revealing experiences. Unlike the deities of Greece, Mesopotamia, or Canaan, the Israelite deity may speak softly, apart from manifestations in nature. While this author is difficult to date, he or she is one who clearly wishes to set Israel's God apart from the gods of its neighbors.

These theophanic scenes reveal certain traditional motifs and clusters of motifs. Reviewing them uncovers not only the experiential expectations of Israelite audiences but also the traditional nature of the literature that frames and expresses them. God may be experienced in the power of nature or, as in 1 Kings 19, set apart from, over, and above the sound and fury of the natural realm. God is covenant partner, protector, and confidant as the majestic scenes filled with special sounds and sights finally focus on an intimate cameo featuring God and human. The receivers of covenant and related divine charges are all men. A different theophany is reserved especially for the experiences of women.

Annunciation

The background of this particular theophanic form is the birth or youth of a male hero. Barrenness of the mother or endangerment of the child are recurring markers of the future importance of the child. In such instances the deity or a divine emissary sometimes gives instructions to the mother or mother-to-be, always assuring her that a child will be born and will prosper as blessed by God. The fathers in these situations are secondary to their wives; the women are the primary receivers of the divine message and experience. It is perhaps a mark of the androcentric orientations of the framers of the Hebrew Bible and of their worldviews that some of the few instances in which women encounter God have to do with their role or would-be roles as mothers, for the male deity is the one who opens and closes the womb (Gen. 30:2, 1 Sam. 1:5).

Annunciation scenes involve Sarah (Genesis 18), Hagar (Gen. 16: 7–14, 21:8–21) and Rebekah (Gen. 25:22–23). The revelation to Hagar raises important issues in biblical ethics. Hagar has been sent away with her son by Abraham, whose wife Sarah wishes her son Isaac to have no rival. The theological frame of the narrative suggests that Sarah (like Rebekah after her) knows God's will, that Isaac the younger is to inherit his father's mantle (21:12). In a sense, Sarah's annunciation leads her to attempt to limit the rights of another would-be hero whose mother will receive her own revelations. So God's choice intermingles with the traditional folktale pattern concerning the successes of the younger son. Such a passage, however, prods the modern reader (as well as the classical rabbis) to worry about God's fairness and about Abraham's excessive passivity. It almost comes as no surprise that he would sacrifice Isaac (chapter 22). The annunciation scene, however, portrays Yahweh as intervening to protect the boy Ishmael from harm. He hears his cry, speaks with comforting words to the mother, and makes a well of water spring up in the wilderness (Gen. 21:17–19). The mother is able to give the boy water. God is manifested in a voice and in the capacity to bring forth sources of fertility from the arid surroundings.

In a lengthier scene of annunciation, a divine man reveals to a barren woman, the wife of Manoah, that the hero Samson is to be born (Judges 13). This scene is rich in the motifs of the experiential. An angel whose appearance is like that of the angel of God—exceedingly awe-inspiring, a human "man of God" and yet divine—asks, "Why do you ask my name, seeing it is wonderful?" (Judges 13:6,18) The fire, the sign of God, appears miraculously to consume Manoah's offering. An important thread in the theophany called annunciation that emerges with particular force in Judges 13 is the savvy persona of the unnamed woman, in contrast to her frightened, uncertain husband. The divine figure communicates first and most completely with the woman. The man doubts his wife's reports, asks for more information, and finally fears that the power of the divine will burst forth destructively upon them. The woman knows that the power has come in peace and with blessings. The annunciation is the woman's theophany; it is probably male-generated, perhaps patronizing in its implications for modern women, but it is nevertheless an empowering cameo of the experiential for women within the contours of an androcentric worldview.

Other Encounters on Earth: Personal Passages

Another set of experiential scenes involves male heroes' encounters with the deity at critical life passages. One such scene involves the quintessential trickster Jacob, ancestor-hero of the Israelites. Having stolen his elder brother Esau's birthright and his blessing, with his mother Rebekah's continuing help he flees from the vengeance of Esau to Rebekah's family in Paddam-aram. Lying down upon the earth to sleep at night, a stone serving as his pillow, he dreams and beholds a ladder reaching from earth to heaven, the angels of God ascending and descending upon it (Gen. 28:10–17). The Lord himself appears and reiterates the promises of his covenant with the descendants of Abraham, Isaac, and Jacob: land and progeny and God's protective presence. Jacob awakens and is described as filled with fear and awe, recognizing that he has been allowed to see "the house of God," "the gate of heaven" (Gen. 28:17). He names the place Bethel, "the house of God," as the cameo scene becomes an etiology for a city's name.

In the larger life history of Jacob that is one of the rich narrative threads of Genesis, this experience of the numinous marks a rite of passage and signals a process of transformation as the hero moves away from his homeland to confront new challenges, marry, raise children, and assert his own identity. The passage, moreover, reemphasizes the special relationship between God and Israel, here represented by her ancestor-hero, the father of the twelve tribes.

The Israelite composer delves into a universal set of motifs that human beings associate with experiences of the heavenly realm. Ladders to heaven are found in the tales of diverse cultures including those of Native Americans and Africans as humanly comprehensible items of hardware or fixtures of the natural realm, such as mountains, are imagined to link us with a beyond. Such imagery testifies to the need to see beyond our limited reality, to establish a connectedness with some sort of ultimate. In this Israelite imagining, the "navel of the universe" intertwines with specific Israelite national aspirations for the homeland and for security and fecundity within its borders.

Such a description of the experiential could appeal to an Israelite of any period. During the early monarchy such a scene would make sense of and justify Israel's empire. During the exile such a scene keeps alive hopes of renewal and restoration, for the land was promised to Jacob at the center of the universe where heaven meets earth. The presence of angels also seems to imply an author who imagines Yahweh surrounded and accompanied by a retinue of heavenly beings, a motif we will see in a host of other scenes of the experiential. God is not alone in heaven but, like any king divine or human, has a large support staff. Such images go back millennia in ancient Near Eastern portrayals of the deity and are continued in the religion of Yahweh, in which one particular deity dominates.

As Jacob's departure from Israel is marked by an experience of God, so is his return. Here Jacob's rite of passage leads to reconciliation with Esau and to an assumption of his hard-won, God-sanctioned place as head of his patrilineage. This scene at the Jabboq River is one of the eeriest and most enigmatic in Scripture and provides insight into views of the deity that differ from the transcendent, suprahuman covenant partner of Genesis 12, 15, and 17 and Exodus 3, 6, and 19. It is significant that for the Israelite writers who compiled Genesis, times of psychological stress and life-altering decisions coincide with experiences of the numinous. It is at such flash points that the heavens may open, that one seeks a sign, that the world seems out of kilter and extraordinary. Transformation is thus perceived in many cultures. And as a piece of the national myth, the experience of the individual becomes the shared experience of the community.

After Jacob's family crosses the river, he remains behind. The lonely setting by the river, the night, and the sense of solitude create the atmosphere for transformation and the experiential. A "man" is said to wrestle with him until morning. Jacob holds his ground even though he is injured. At daybreak the being implores to be released. "Let go of me, for the dawn is rising" (Gen. 32:26). Jacob demands a blessing and receives a new name. The folk etymology identifies him as one who perseveres with God and humans (32:29) and endures. The "man" refuses to give his own name. Perhaps it is obvious ("Why do you ask my name, seeing it is wonderful?" [Judg. 13:18]). Perhaps he does not not want to give Jacob more power over him, for the name is the person, and to know the name is to control the person (cf.

Rumpelstiltskin). But Jacob realizes that he has "seen God face to face" (32:31) and survived.

In this passage the deity is threatening, a demon of sorts, a river spirit. Moses has a comparable encounter with a destroyer deity as he returns to Egypt to fulfill his calling as the enslaved Israel's rescuer (Exod. 4:24–26). In this strange nocturnal scene at a way station, Moses is saved by his wife's quick action. She cuts off the foreskin of their son and touches Moses' feet (possibly a euphemism for the genitals). The blood wards off (or satisfies) Yahweh in this aggressive and demonic guise.

Such experiences of the aggressively numinous reveal much about the Israelites' notions of self-transformation and confirm their belief in the potential for encounters with the power of divinity. These scenes also provide a fascinating portrait of the deity that markedly contrasts with the divine warrior, the strong, transcendent leader, the father, and the judge seen elsewhere. Scholars frequently assign the "demon portraits" to an early period in Israel's history, the pre-state days before the monarchy; or, alternatively, they suggest that such portraits appealed to the "popular" tradition as opposed to the sophisticated, mainstream classical tradition. According to this line of reasoning, the demons are carryovers that for one reason or another have survived in the canon. Such an approach fails to take account of the richness of Israelite religion manifested in the biblical tradition. Clearly God was viewed through many lenses and in many guises. Israelites were capable of imagining encounters with God in various physical dimensions. God has the capacity to be dangerous, and portrayals of the deity are complex and conflicting. Human beings' relationship with God is often seen as a struggle.

The Heavenly Realm

These examples of the experiential dimension all involve imaginings of the appearance of God or his emissary on earth. In another set of encounters, human beings are transported to the realm of God. The simplest scene of the heavenly realm is found in Exodus 24 as Moses, Aaron, Nadab, Abihu, and seventy of the elders of Israel "go up" and behold the God of Israel. "Under his (God's) feet there was something like tilework of sapphire, like the substance of heaven for purity. There they did eat and drink and behold the Lord" (24:10). In the Bible's own chronology, this is an "early" scene, the banquet that celebrates Israel's becoming a people at Mount Sinai. Such an image could be as old as Israel itself. Comparable imaginings of the heavenly realm and human transportation thereto are found throughout the world's religions. This is a simple but powerful scene emphasizing the sense of sight. More datable and typologically stylized scenes of the realm of heaven are found in 1 Kings 22:19–22, Isaiah 6, Ezekiel 1–3, and Daniel 7. In each case a seer receives a glimpse of the divinity, who is seated on a throne surrounded by his courtiers, angelic or cherubic beings arranged to his right and to his left. The visionary observes, overhears, or participates in the activities of the divine court. While 1 Kings 22:19–22 presents only a brief cameo in which Micaiah, the prophet, sees the Lord and hears the doom pronounced over the northern Israelite king Ahab (ninth century B.C.E.), the other visions are more elaborate and detailed even while the deity becomes somewhat more veiled and hidden.

Isaiah 6 presents an initiation of the eighth-century B.C.E. prophet Isaiah. In this visionary experience, Isaiah sees the Lord and describes the throne of God and mentions the very hem of his robe. The seraphim cover his face and feet (cf. English/Greek), an act viewed by Eilberg-Schwartz as an indication of Israelite self-conciousness about the nature of God's body (1994:59–80). The seraphs, moreover, chant a hymn to one another extolling the deity's holiness, his sacred and total otherness: "Holy, holy, holy is the Lord of Hosts. The whole earth is filled with his glory" (3). The prophet is cleansed of sin and transformed (cf. Zechariah 3) into a vessel for God's words when his mouth is touched by a coal taken from the altar. The divine realm is a mirror of the earthly temple in Jerusalem, or the latter is a human imitation of God's realm. Finally, the prophet volunteers to deliver God's message, this in contrast to a shyer Moses (Exod. 3:11, 4:10) and Jeremiah (Jer. 1:6).

Ezekiel's sixth-century B.C.E. vision of the divine realm is even more baroque, while the divine figure is also more difficult to discern. The angelic figures are described at length, with a sense of caution and uncertainty. They are "something like four living creatures" (1:5). In the midst of the heavenly creatures is something that looks like burning coals of fire and torches moving to and fro. Lightning issues forth from the fire. Next to these heavenly, barely describable creatures and elements is a sort of chariot, the quintessential icon of postbiblical Jewish mysticism. The opening chapters of Ezekiel, in fact, have come to be regarded as a doorway to the divine realm. The chariot throne was the central iconography of the Jerusalem temple, as the divine realm in Ezekiel mirrors the place where God has caused his spirit to dwell on earth. The whirring wheels look like the gleam of a precious stone (1:16). Again they are not precious stones but look like them. Over the heads of the living creatures there is something spread out like a firmament, a heavenly vault like crystal (1:22). The wings of the heavenly creatures sound like mighty waters, like thunder or the voice of God, a roar like the sound of an armed camp (1:24). Something appears that resembles a throne of sapphire (1:26). This wonderfully tentative description of heavenly surroundings and personnel is matched in ambiguity by the description of the deity. "Above the likeness of a throne was the form of the likeness of a human being" (1:26–28). A "brightness" is mentioned "like the appearance of the bow in a cloud on a rainy day. This was the appearance of the likeness of the glory of the Lord." Notice all the distancing, the explicit approximation. The prophet recognizes that he has encountered the divine, but the experience is dreamlike and not quite concrete (see Wilson 1987:164–67). He falls on his face and hears the voice of someone speaking. He is commanded: "O mortal, stand up on your feet." A spirit enters Ezekiel and he receives God's charge to speak to the people.

Like Isaiah, Ezekiel undergoes a ritual of transformation. He eats a scroll offered to him by the divine being. It is sweet as honey and literally fills him with God's word. Ezekiel is described as filled with God's spirit, lifted up by a spirit (3:12), able to perceive God's glory rise from its place (3:12), able to see the machinations of the divine courtiers and to hear their charge from Yahweh (9:3–7) and to register a protest when he hears the message of doom (9:8). Perhaps more than any biblical prophet, he is portrayed as steeped in the experiential.

Encounter with the Divinely Dead

1 Samuel 28, the scene in which a female spirit medium raises for the King Saul the spirit of the deceased prophet Samuel, reveals another aspect of Israelite images of the experiential. Samuel had anointed Israel's first king and had also conveyed to Saul messages of God's displeasure, predicting his defeat and replacement at the hands of the Judean David, son of Jesse.

This passage provides insight into views of the dead (discussed in chap. 1) that apparently were a vital part of Israelite popular religion. This thread in the tradition is not appreciated by many of the framers of the Hebrew Bible who make it clear that cults of the dead are not, in their view, a proper part of Yahwism (Lev. 19:28). The raising of the dead and implicit accompanying attempts to commune with them are condemned in Deuteronomy (18:11–12) along with divination, child sacrifice, and fertility rites—all related spheres of religious expression, as Susan Ackerman has argued (1992).

Indeed, the frame of this narrative about Saul insists that he, the king, has outlawed necromancy. He comes in disguise to the woman of Endor and asks her to bring forth for him a ghost, the one whom he tells her. She responds, perhaps coyly, that Saul has eliminated the spirit mediums, the ghost seekers, upon penalty of death (1 Sam. 28: 9). Saul swears to her that no sin will fall upon her. She asks, "Whom shall I raise for you?" and Saul responds "Raise for me Samuel" (11).

Unfortunately, the passage does not provide details about the mode in which ancient Israelite spirit mediums work, how they achieve a trancelike state or communion with the spirit world, or how the dead are actually raised. What ritual actions are followed? What modes of descent lead into the realm of the dead? The biblical account is brief yet filled with drama in the expectation of a participatory event. The narrator allows us to observe the woman's experience and causes us to feel her heightened sense of the otherworldly: the woman sees Samuel and screams out in a loud voice, suddenly filled with insight. She demands, "Why did you deceive me, for you are Saul!" Saul calms her and asks her what she sees. She replies, "I see gods rise from the earth." The "gods" (*'elōhîm* or, more frequently, *'ēlîm*) are the souls of the dead, deified in Sheol, having a curiously unenviable immortality like the shades of classical Greek Hades (see chap. 3). Saul and she then concentrate on the demeanor of the beings who apparently emerge from the crowd as the Hebrew switches from the plural in verse 13 to the singular in verse 14. Saul demands, "What is his appearance?" or perhaps "What does it all look like?," and she responds "An old man is rising up, and he is wrapped in a robe." Saul then knows it to be Samuel and reverently "bows, his face to the ground, and prostrates himself" (14).

Samuel, the crusty old prophet, no more accommodating to Saul in death than in life, conveys to Saul God's continuing displeasure and prophesies the king's imminent demise in battle, a reliable prophecy backed by the ageless knowledge of the otherworld.

The woman's role as a mediator in this passage is notable, as is its literary location in the epic of Saul, no less compelling in drama and placement than Hamlet's encounter with the ghost of his father or Odysseus's consultation with Tiresias. The powerful character of Samuel lives on beyond death. The narrator as creative writer could not bear to let him go, but the fact that he need not says something about the Israelites' views of death and the ongoing involvement of the dead in their lives, for good or evil, permitting yet other opportunities for the experiential.

Israelite conceptions of the ways in which human beings experience the divine are vibrant and varied, emerging in several favorite conventionalized literary topoi that allow their narrators considerable flexibility and creative license. Certain motifs are pervasive, such as God's association with fire and the power to transform nature through her own violent manifestations in storm and earthquake. Recurring patterns include scenes of covenant-making for men and annunciation scenes for women. The divine council has a set configuration as well. These examples of the experiential both reflect and help shape essential threads in Israelite worldview: the notion of Israel's special relationship with God in which each partner, divine and human, has certain rights and responsibilities; the quintessential notion of Yahweh as creator of the world and all living beings; and the belief that the dead live on in an underworld existence, implying their capacity to continue to help or hurt us. Rachel weeps for her children, evoking God's forgiveness and a promise of release (Jer. 31:15), while Samuel brings a message to an individual ruler concerning his doom. God dwells in a parallel realm, a king surrounded by courtiers, but lucky mortals may at times join the council's meetings. The power of the divine is involved in life-cycle transitions. The God-power may be sought after, but it may also descend unexpectedly, marking the assumption of new statuses and responsibilities and signaling a significant moment in the biography of a hero.

Can one match the various traditional scenes of the experiential with particular periods in Israelite history as delineated in chapter 1? Some of the experiences previously described, such as the raising of the dead on demand, appear to be the purview of professionals in this as in other cultures. Concepts of the dead as "gods" and notions about life after death were probably popular among Israelites throughout their history, significantly predating fully developed concepts of bodily resurrection that would emerge by the second century B.C.E.

Scenes of covenant-making belong to men, their realm being that of public interaction. Indeed, even at Mount Sinai, those addressed are commanded not to touch women sexually (Exod. 19:15), implying that the divine message is conveyed to and through men.

Some scholars have viewed the two covenant scenes in Genesis (chaps. 15 and 17) and Exodus (chaps. 3 and 6) as entries in the "J" and "P" sources or documents discussed in chapter 1. Others have suggested that the promise of land so prominent in covenant scenes comes not as part of an early foundation mythology but from exilic writers, justifying their divine rights to the land and consequently their hopes for its reclamation. I suggest that the covenant scenes reflect a lengthy and complex trajectory in Israelite literature and culture. It does seem clear that what an author does with the topos (e.g., whether covenant is conditional or unconditional, whether God is in the upturning of nature or a voice apart) says much about his own view of the deity and the ways in which God relates to Israel and individual Israelites. The tradition offers considerable variation and no simple evolutionary scheme.

Similarly, while some would see Jacob's and Moses' encounters with a demonic deity as primitive carryovers of popular religion, the very inclusion of such texts in Scripture implies the continuing meaningfulness of such descriptions of the experiential to Israelites even at the close of the biblical period.

The scenes of the divine council do evidence a datable stylistic development over time from less to more baroque. Similarly, whereas the simple imagery in Exod. 24:10 and 1 Kings 22:19 could come from even the earliest period in Israelite history, the scene in Isaiah 6 and the opening chapters of Ezekiel are written with the great temple in Jerusalem and its iconography in mind, though the temple, like the earlier tabernacle, was clearly regarded by Israelites as based on the heavenly realm. The very design of these holy places, according to threads in the tradition, was specified in other visionary experiences of God (Exod. 25:9, 31:3–4, 1 Chron. 28:19).

SUGGESTED READINGS

In addition to Ninian Smart's discussion of the experiential in his two books, classic discussions of the ways in which human beings experience the otherworldly and divine are Otto's *The Idea of the Holy* (1928) and Eliade's *Shamanism* (1964). With specific reference to Israelite and Jewish literature, see my essay on the visionary in *Ideal Figures in Ancient Judaism* (1980) and my book *The Symbolic Vision in Biblical Tradition* (1980).

The motif of the threatening deity is discussed by Eliade in *Shamanism*. The specific biblical scenes are explored in my book *Underdogs and Tricksters* (1987) and in works by Irvin and Hendel.

The annunciation scene is explored in some detail by Alter in a larger discussion of biblical type scenes in *The Art of Biblical Narrative* (1981), by Exum, and by me in the commentary on Genesis in *The Women's Bible Commentary* (1992).

Issues concerning God's body are creatively explored in Eilberg-Schwartz's *God's Phallus* (1994).

3

Where From, Where To?: Mythic Patterns of Origins and Death

Perhaps the most pervasive and well-studied pattern in Israelite literature describes the creation of the cosmos. Cosmogony, or world creation, deals with the ways in which order supplants chaos and productive fertility comes to replace the power of sterility. Neglected until recently, is another biblical mythic complex that addresses what happens to humans beings after they die, their encounter with the underworld and the shades who have died before them. In some threads of the ancient Israelite tradition, these two fundamental, value-laden complexes intertwine and overlap in interesting ways. As a means of entering the "mythic dimension" of religion, I will examine each of these themes in turn and explore the ways in which notions of world creation and of human mortality inform one another.

Every traditional culture partakes of creation myth, one or more essential stories that describe how life began. Such stories not only impart information to the curious but also provide value-rich metaphysical guides to the very workings of the world and explain the place of human beings within it. Creation mythology offers a community a sense of shared identity, a picture of its earliest context. It is important to know about one's primordial roots in order to understand current realities.

From Chaos to Cosmos

On a very basic level, creation myths unite all of us. It is quite remarkable how shared images are used by humans of various cultures to describe a time of primordial chaos before the world's ordering and creation: darkness; lack of differentiation among physical features of the universe; infertile waters; emptiness; formlessness; and the absence of life. With creation comes an ordered, peopled world, physical definition, a calendar, and a possibility for growth and change. Scholars offer various explanations for the shared imagery, some suggesting that all human beings are born with a set of symbolic templates, archetypal images that are part of our psychic nature as humans, while others claim that the story of creation was first told somewhere and then spread, like humankind, over wide geographic areas. In any case, this essential pattern finds more culturally bound expressions in specific traditions.

In the ancient Near East, the typical story in which the passage from chaos to cosmos is imagined describes a mighty battle. The great Mesopotamian creation epic Enuma elish, whose name consists of the narrative's first words ("When above"), provides a fine example. Enuma elish describes world creation as occurring in two stages. First comes an early theogonic time when all that exists are the initial couple, the god Apsu identified with the sweet water and the goddess Tiamat identified with the sea, and their son Mummu, a god who is the mist that rises from the waters (see Heidel 1951:3). At first "their waters mingled together / And no pasture land had been formed [and] not [even] a reed marsh was to be seen" (1:5–7). In the Mesopotamian version of primeval chaos, as in other versions, imagery is of nondifferentiation and formlessness.

Apsu and Tiamat beget a series of additional primeval pairs of gods, for example, Lahmu and Lahamu, who have been interpreted as male and female personifications of silt, and Anshar and Kishar, male and female manifestations of the horizon (see Jacobsen 1968:185). In turn, these pairs have children, the most important in their line being Ea the wise and eventually his son Marduk.

The begetting of children by the primeval gods already sets into motion the process of change which is at the heart of world creation, the second stage in the creation of the cosmos. The transformative crisis occurs when the young gods make so much noise that their elders cannot sleep. Apsu determines to destroy them but is eliminated by his crafty descendant Ea. Tiamat, who apparently held her peace when her children killed Apsu (1:113), is later shamed into avenging him. The recurring language of the traditional-style epic describes her as monstrous, fierce, and threatening. Her decrees are "powerful" and "irresistible" (3:93). She is mother-chaos, the sea, "raging," "furious," and "frenzied" (3:73–74, 4:76, 88), threatening to devour those she has created. This time it is Marduk, the powerful young god, who defeats her with magic weapons. After his victory, Marduk takes Tiamat's carcass, splits it in half like a mussel, and creates the cosmos out of the parts, turning the procreative wild stuff of her into a productive world order. The process of cosmogony continues with the creation of the calendar and the heavenly bodies, and the formation of humankind out of the blood of Tiamat's general Kingu. Finally, Marduk builds his palace or sanctuary (6:57) Babylon, the political and cultural center of the bearers of this creation tradition, a center of the universe in the author's worldview.

The movement from chaos to order, from nondifferentiation to categories and stations, emerges in a traditional epic-war pattern. This is story, riveting and engaging, including an initial threat, the emergence of a hero, the preparation of special weapons, the battle and the victory, the building of the hero's "house," which is the world, and finally the celebratory banquet. This essential plot means creation throughout the ancient Near Eastern and Mediterranean world. One could cite additional examples drawn from the Greek tradition preserved in Hesiod's *Theogony* and, closer to Israel, from the fourteenth-century B.C.E.

Canaanite city-state of Ugarit, in which world creation is a version of this story. The same narrative pattern or sections of it expressed creation in ancient Israel, and yet echoes of the pattern are faint in Genesis 1 and 2, the opening creation myths of the Bible.

Certainly, Genesis 1 and 2 both include the essential transformation from chaos to cosmos. Indeed, the unproductive "Deep" covered by darkness in Genesis 1 is the Hebrew term *těhôm*, a cognate of the Akkadian Tiamat. Images of primordial waters are found in both Genesis 1 and 2, the latter presenting chaos as a misty bog. Like Enuma elish, Genesis 1 includes pairs of early elements: Earth/Sky; *Tōhû/Bōhû* (the latter might be translated as "Emptiness/Void"). The very order of what is created and ordered parallels Marduk's activities after his defeat of the goddess. One might well suggest that the authors of Genesis 1 and Enuma elish share a more geographically specific version of creation, but where is the battle?

In Genesis 1 all is accomplished through the magisterial word of God, which is immediate, powerful, and unchallenged. The very style of the passage, with its solid, architectonic repeating frames, reinforces this impression of certainty. Creation proceeds day by day until the Creator rests on the Sabbath. It has been suggested that this composition is a priestly work because of its elegant scholastic style and the climactic emphasis on the Sabbath. While it is certainly true that Genesis 1 is a monumental, sophisticated, and majestic tale, perhaps reflecting an urbane or aristocratic sort of writer for whom the Sabbath is ethnically and religiously self-defining, he or she need not be a priest. I believe the writer is exilic or postexilic, however, drawing a distinction between the Israelites and their neighbors through the version of creation employed, a writer concerned to define "us" as not "them." Our God is one, while theirs are multiple. Our God need only speak and the world becomes, theirs need to fight. The version of creation found in Genesis 1 points to Israelite insecurity at a time when her people, holy city, and temple have been conquered by the Babylonians, the people of Marduk. In fact, many Israelites feared that Yahweh was weak, no longer able to protect his people, no longer God. Genesis 1 answers boldly, as does the contemporaneous work

Isaiah 40, that God is the sole creator and is all-powerful. No tension grips the reader of Genesis 1, for chaos has no power. Rather, one approaches the account in awe, in the mode of the experiential.

Genesis 2 presents a less majestic God. He plants a garden like a farmer, molds his human creation like a sculptor, blows life into him like a glassblower, and yet even in this passage from the infertile and undifferentiated world to one that is divided by primeval rivers, productively planted, and inhabited by a variety of creatures, God is the sole creator and does not come to power in a war story.

This cosmogony is more down to earth in style, tone, and content than Genesis 1, its deity less transcendent. In fact, world creation in Genesis 2 serves as a prelude to the more interesting tale about the emergence of reality outside the garden in Genesis 3, the famous story about God, the man, the woman, and the snake that is integral to the creation account in Genesis 2–3. In this continuation of the cosmogonic process, the humans break a prohibition not to eat from God's tree, the tree of knowledge of good and evil. Ironically, once they become like the gods, knowing good and evil, they are expelled from an ideal, a harmonious paradise, into the toils and tribulations of reality with its work roles and hierarchies. And yet reality is not inexorably evil. The Israelite writer does not describe "a fall" but rather a passage into the world as he or she and the audience lived it. Knowing the origins of one's condition makes it more acceptable, even while the imagery of Eden provides a model for how things might have been and, for some biblical writers, a model for a future, eagerly awaited time.

Genesis 2–3 is not as grand or elegant in style and sweep as Genesis 1 and Enuma elish. Genesis 2–3 provides a timeless comment on the nature of being human in God's world. It images a God who walks in the garden he has planted and who fears the potential power of the humans to become too godlike. He is not in absolute control of all he has created and, like the great gods Thor or Zeus, is tricked or disobeyed by those under him (by Loki, Prometheus, and the snake). Nevertheless, he can sweep his creations out of the garden once the chicanery is uncovered and the threats to his power are more bothersome than earth-shaking. Chaos never really has a chance.

An alternate creation cluster that shares some of the "battlelessness" of the account found in Genesis 1 is preserved in Proverbs. This creation material is of special interest because of the role played by Wisdom, the goddesslike hypostatization who accompanies Yahweh, his veritable aide-de-camp or perhaps even his consort. Whereas other ancient Near Eastern creation traditions do feature creative goddesses in a prominent role (e.g., the Mesopotamian Mami), the biblical tradition of the Israelites features the male deity. It is he who creates and shapes the world, he who can bring back the flood in Genesis 6–9 and cause it to recede, he who opens and closes the womb of the female humans descended from the woman he originally fashioned from the male's rib and the male he formed from dust. Folklorists have suggested that the Israelites' version of the deity betrays a certain womb-envy. So, too, does the Babylonian version, in which Marduk breaks the fecund water of the mother goddess to bring forth the cosmos (see Dundes 1988:171).

In Proverbs 8, Wisdom declares that she was "obtained" before the beginning of the earth. The Hebrew term *qnh* literally means "to get" or "to acquire" and is the term used in ancient Hebrew for "marriage." Reinforcing Karl Marx's feminist observation that in patriarchal cultures women were among man's first moveable possessions, one acquires or "buys" a wife as one buys cattle. In fact, the first person soliloquy of Lady Wisdom extols her as a vitally important force, the only one who observed God's formation of the universe. In this account there is a time before there were depths (*těhōmôt* [24]; note again the use of the cognate to Tiamat, as in Genesis 1). This account makes chaos even less of an independent force than in Genesis 1, where the waters preexist in some sense. In Proverbs 8, cosmic order is perceived in terms of shaping mountains, literally stamping them out (25) as with a cookie cutter; the earth is created, the heaven established (26–27). In an evocation of the battle-with-sea version of creation, Wisdom declares she observed God-set limits, literally his law, upon the sea so that the water dare not transgress his word. Proverbs 8:28 might be translated "when the fountains of the deep grew fierce" in an overt allusion to the familiar mythic theme. Wisdom sees all of this and participates, a master builder by God's side, daily his delight, "sporting" before him always, a term that often has erotic connotations (8:30). Wisdom plays or sports (31) in the world at large. Powerful, primordial, and playful, Wisdom is God's missing wife, a witness to the coming of the cosmos, the process by which the deeps are safely bounded. In Proverbs 9, echoes of the victory–enthronement creation pattern continue with Wisdom herself at its productive center. It is she who builds her house. (Recall Marduk's building of Babylon and the Canaanite god Baal's house, built with windows after his victories over the forces of Chaos.) It is Wisdom who makes the victory banquet and sends servant girls to invite guests. In the beautiful metaphor of Proverbs, it is wisdom she offers. These are her "bread and wine" (5), for it is upon Wisdom that all creation rests.

It is difficult to date Proverbs 8–9. Most scholars view it as a late biblical tour de force richly informed by the more ageless mythic pattern found in versions throughout the ancient Near East. Proverbs 8–9 is the work of a sophisticated, urbane writer who comes closer than any other biblical writer to describing the goddess, one who is thus not uncomfortable with the idea of the male creator's consort being directly involved in the cosmogonic process and essential to it. And yet the use of the battle-with-sea motif is subtle and theologically quite controlled in Proverbs 8–9 as it is in Genesis 1.

Other Israelites, familiar with versions of creation that describe an exciting defeat of chaos, express worldview in a battle tale, understanding the way and origins of the cosmos in the medium of such a narrative pattern. Many of the passages that reveal the use of the theme of victory over chaos in its more typical ancient Near Eastern form are probably from the same period as Genesis 1, the time of the exile. Various biblical writers embrace this ancient myth to describe Yahweh's power and his implicit or explicit capacity to rescue his people. The victory against chaos assures them in the words of the prophet 2 Isaiah that God did not create the world to be a chaos, a Tohu (45: 18). Chaos continues to threaten in the form of war, death, sickness, sterility, evil, and storm, but Yahweh has power over all.

Nuances of the so-called victory–enthronement creation pattern emerge in Israel's very founding myth. The escape from the tyrant

es of defeating chaos, which is often
of the plagues in Exodus 7–12 builds
nages of new chaos, an overturning of
out in Genesis 1: blood runs not safely
beings but defiles the rivers; frogs exist
overrun the land as proper boundaries
day and night; wild beasts break from the
of human civilization; finally death itself,
station, claims the lives of Egypt's first-born
it this upon his world through his hubris and
rite; now God will not let him escape even if
15 Pharaoh speaks the haughty taunts of the
aders know of his defeat.

ill pursue. I will overtake.
ill divide the spoil.
y appetite will have its fill of them.
will draw my sword.
My hand will dispossess of them.
(Exod. 15:9)

ythm of the ancient poetry captures in brief strokes
of the warrior; one is made to feel in the texture of his
renalin of the enemy, already savoring his victory.
n of the challenge motif is paired with allusions to battle
in Exod. 15:1–8, 11–12, and 14–16a. Nuances of the vic-
sion are found at verses 13 and 16b, and of the enthrone-
rses 17–18. The people are established in God's abode, the
n" of the Lord's possession, Yahweh's sanctuary—an allusion
to the holy land, Zion, or to Mount Sinai, where God will
l and make a covenant in Exodus 19–20. In the pre-monarchic
ncentralized culture that gave rise to this early poem, the sanc-
or abode may have been perceived as a more poetic and less
fied reference to a cosmic center of Israel's universe made man-
in various earthly places where God was believed to cause his
rit to dwell. The formation of the people Israel thus takes place in
e literary framework of world-creation, no less important or funda-

mental is this creation than the initial ordering of the co
myth of God's creation of his people Israel in a miraculous
the sea, through the sea, is also recalled in Joshua 3–4, wh
scholars view as an allusion to an early ritual when Israelite
their founding myth in a processional crossing of the Jorda
The victory in the sea also becomes closely identified in Isra
dition with the victory over the sea as people creation becom
more overtly synonymous with world creation.

> When Israel went out from Egypt
> the house of Jacob from a people who babble in strange languag
> Judah became his sanctuary
> Israel his domain
> The sea looked and fled
> The Jordan turned back
> The mountains skipped about like rams
> the hills like lambs
> What is the matter with you, Sea, that you flee,
> Jordan that you turn back,
> mountains that you skip about like rams,
> hills like lambs?   (Ps. 114:1–1)

God's role as faithful covenant partner rests upon the ancient traditio
of God the mighty warrior-creator. Indeed, all significant roles i
which Yahweh is involved with Israel—protector, selector of kings
rescuer, and lawgiver—intertwine with this primeval role of the deity
as creator who defeats the forces of chaos, frequently personified as a
watery monster (e.g., Rahab, Leviathan, the dragon, the River, the
Sea).

In a Judahite psalm from the period of the monarchy that reiterates
the promise to David and his descendants, (Ps. 89:1–37), Yahweh is
recalled as follows:

> You rule the swelling of the sea
> when its waves rise, you still them
> You crushed Rahab like a carcass
> with your mighty arm
> you scattered your enemies
>   (10–11)

David, whose power is to be granted by God (19) as eternal (29–37), indeed becomes godlike in his own capacity to rule the sea, to control the river (25). The selection of David, in turn, is seen as part and parcel of the very creation of the world, inevitable and essential to Israelite self-identity. The pro-Davidic material in Ps. 89:1–37 has been filled out by later messages in Ps. 89:38–52. The historical context of the latter, like that of Psalm 74, is the difficult time of the late monarchy or the exile, when chaos again threatens. God is reminded of his power in creation and of his promise (49–51). In this way a pro-Davidic paean, set in terms of creation, becomes a means of inspiring the deity to act, to recreate on Israel's behalf.

Writing at the time of the calamitous confrontation with Babylon, the prophet Habakkuk describes a vision he has had of the warrior deity come to save the people and crush her enemies:

> Against the rivers did you burn with rage, O Yahweh
> Was it against the rivers, your anger
> Was it against the sea, your overflowing fury
> When you mounted your horses, your chariots of salvation
> (Hab. 3:8)

The plane of history and the plane of primeval war converge as the ancient mythic pattern speaks to the prophet's present fears and hopes. Another psalmist composes the following:

> You shattered the Sea by your might
> You broke the heads of the dragons in the water
> You crushed the heads of Leviathan
> You gave him as food for the ship-faring folk
> You split open springs and torrents
> You dried up ever-flowing rivers
> Yours is the day, yours also the night
> You established the moon and the sun
> You have set all the boundaries of the earth
> Summer and winter you fashioned.
> (Ps. 74:13–17)

This beautiful and brief Israelite "Enuma elish" is set within a late-monarchic or exilic-period hymn that asks where God the mighty creator is, now that his people need him. "How long, O God, is the foe to taunt?" the psalmist asks (10). It is as if the Israelite writer wishes to remind Yahweh of his power and himself of the ultimate possibility for vindication and restoration. (In a similar vein, see Ps. 77:16–20 and Ps. 89:38–52.)

In a dramatic layering of ancient Near Eastern creation myth, Israelite foundation myth, and a contemporary community's hopes, the sixth-century B.C.E. prophet-poet Deutero-Isaiah addresses his warrior:

> Awake, awake, clothe yourself with strength,
> O arm of the Lord
> Awake as in days of old
> the generations of long ago!
> Was it not you who hewed up Rahab
> who pierced the dragon?
> Was it not you who dried up the sea
> the waters of the great deep
> who made the depths of the sea a path
> for the redeemed to cross?
> So the ransomed of Yahweh will return
> and come to Zion with singing
> eternal joy upon their heads;
> exultation and gladness, they will attain [or will reach them]
> and sorrow and sighing will flee away.
>
>   (Isa. 51:9–11)

What the Israelite composer himself or herself considers to be ancient, primordial times is thus juxtaposed with Israel's ancient history to speak directly to the present situation of listeners. Once again the Israelite author seeks to rouse the divine warrior as if from slumber or depression with memories of his greatest victories, his capacity to create and transform.

And yet even these powerful passages do not fully convey the range of stories about God's victory over chaos which must have been recounted among the Israelites. Job, the sixth-century B.C.E. story of the righteous sufferer who contends with God, alludes to some of these tales in describing the ultimate power of God. A general reference to the story of the victory over the sea, similar to those cited earlier, occurs in Job 26:12: "By his power he disturbed the Sea; by his understanding he smote through Rahab." To God is attributed the youthful power associated with Marduk and the wisdom associated with Ea in Mesopotamian religion.

To convey an image of God's conquering anger, which Job believes God has turned against him, the author writes: "God will not turn back his anger; beneath him bowed the helpers of Rahab" (9:13). Like Tiamat, Rahab had her underlings and cohorts whom Yahweh brings to submission. The sea at Job 38:8–11 is imagined to be conquered and bound, its potential fury is tamed and made a useful and productive part of an orderly, God-created, controlled cosmos. The fullest narrative is found at Job 41:1–13, a passage that gives a real sense of some of the ways in which an Israelite singer of tales might craft his creation epic.

Chapter 41 consists of a series of rhetorical questions posed by the deity from within the whirlwind to declare his awesome power to the mere mortal who has summoned him. Each question reveals a bit more about the traditional tale of God's conquest of watery chaos. In this version he is called Leviathan (41:1 [Hebrew 40:25]). When God conquers him, he takes him prisoner, "pressing down his tongue" (lit. "making his tongue sink with a chord"), putting a rope of twisted rushes in his nose, and piercing his jaw with a hook or fetter (41:2, [Hebrew 40:26]). The conquered monster begs the conqueror to take him as his servant, implicitly to spare him (41:3–4 [Hebrew 40:27–28]). But the deity can play with him like a captured bird, a pet for his girls; he can allow him to be bargained over and divided up among merchants (5–6 [Hebrew 40:29–30]); he can spear Leviathan like a big fish (7 [Hebrew 40:31]). Only Yahweh can make such battle. Leviathan himself is described as a mighty fire-breathing dragon of "elegant" dimensions (12 [Hebrew 41:4]), having a double jaw (13 [Hebrew 41:5]), with "terror all around its teeth" (14 [Hebrew 41:6]), "eyes like eyelids of the dawn" (18 [Hebrew 41:10]), flaming torches issuing forth from its mouth (19 [Hebrew 41:11]), smoke from its nostrils (20 [Hebrew 41:12]), stirring up the living dead (or gods) (25 [Hebrew 41:17]), impervious to weaponry (26–29 [Hebrew 41:18–21]), making "the deep boil like a pot" (31 [Hebrew 41:23]). This is the rich description of epic, a window on an elaborate traditional narrative theme in the hands of a gifted composer.

The battle–creation pattern also becomes a vehicle in the late-biblical genre called apocalyptic. Writers of apocalypses consider the workaday world on the plane of history to have become a chaos, either because of a group's political persecution, a sense of cultural anomie, or some more specific—perhaps imagined, perhaps personal—reason for believing that time is out of joint. New chaos, however, means that new creation will follow, a paradise of some variety to accompany the laying down of a new and better world order. Chaos need not always be imagined as watery or dragonlike, though sometimes it is in these late, post-monarchic texts. In the second-century B.C.E. symbolic vision of Daniel 7, four beasts emerge from a churned up sea, each a dreamlike combination of animals (e.g., a bearlike creature with three tusks, a leopardlike creature with wings). These beasts represent some of the major superpowers of ancient Near Eastern history, the conquerors and oppressors of Israel. They are defeated in judgment (11), as the depressing sequence of enemy rulers is ended and a new, eternal kingdom for the "people of the holy ones of the Most High" is established (27). The background for this vision of world-shaping is the period of persecution under Antiochus Epiphanes that would lead to the successful Maccabean revolt of 167 B.C.E.

Other significant appearances of the cosmogonic battle appear in works of the late sixth and early fifth centuries, such as Ezekiel 38–39 ("the battle with Gog of Magog") and Zechariah 9 and 14, where the motifs of world creation as a victory over chaos continue to inform and shape the Israelites' conception of struggle and renewal, the alienation of various sectors of the community and their hopes for redefinition.

The creative dialectic—from murky yet often aggressive chaos to constructively productive order—is thus a universal one, specified in ancient Near Eastern thought in the victory–enthronement pattern, specified further in individual Israelite versions. These Israelite scenes portray Yahweh as divine warrior and protagonist and invoke or explain various Israelites' conceptions of their own history, their current reality, and their hopes for the future. We have seen the pattern used to extol kingship in a monarchic-period piece, to comfort exiles in post-monarchic compositions, to describe the eternal grandeur of God's capacity as creator in contrast to our own mundane and limited status, and in apocalyptic works as a means of describing God's meta-historical overturning of current reality, which has itself become a chaos.

It is indeed in such apocalyptic musings that themes of death and chaos often converge, although as the Canaanite epic of Baal and Anat indicates, death is another manifestation of chaos. This narrative has what folklorists would call two "moves," two major plot sequences. In the first Baal defeats Prince Yam, a water-as-chaos equivalent to Tiamat, and then builds his palace. Baal puts windows in the palace, which is the cosmos in the world creation pattern, and Death, Mot, swoops down upon him and drags him to the underworld, Death's domain. In a theme familiar to Westerners from the Greek tale of Persephone, the land becomes sterile, the wadis cease to flow, and the land suffers drought and desolation. Anat, Baal's sister, rescues the god in a second battle-victory cluster, and fertile creation and productivity are reestablished on earth. It is no coincidence that the battle with death and death's defeat become common in a version of the victory–enthronement creation pattern in late-biblical Judaism. Death, as chaos, chaos as death is humankind's eternal enemy. What are the Israelites' attitudes toward death as revealed in their literature? How do these tally with archaeological evidence about burial sites? How is death, as part of the process of chaos-to-cosmos, incorporated into a recurring topos that is a variation upon the victory–enthronement creation pattern?

The Unenviable Immortality

As noted in chapters 1 concerning burial sites and 2 concerning the woman of Endor's raising of the spirit of Samuel in a dramatic and biblically unique example of the experiential, Israelites generally did believe in some sort of "life" after death. This is not to say they believed in bodily resurrection until near the close of the biblical era, nor that notions of existence in the realm of the dead, Sheol, were uniform, but as in Greek tradition the human who died moved on to a shadelike existence in an underworld across the river (Job 33:18). Most descriptions of that existence emphasize a terminal and depressing egalitarianism among the dead, confined to this gloomy, shadowy realm for eternity.

In a dirge over the king of Babylon that is a message of doom designed to bring about the enemy's demise, an oracle in Isaiah 14 declares that Babylon will "be brought down to Sheol, to the recesses of the Pit" (Isa. 14:15). All will gape at him and ask, "Is this the man that made the earth quake? Who made kingdoms shake" (16)?

> Sheol from below rumbles towards you
> to greet your coming.
> It rouses the shades for you
> all the nobles of the earth.
> It raises from their thrones
> all the kings of the nations.
> They all respond and say to you,
> "Even you have become as weak as we
> You are like us.
> Your majesty has been brought down to Sheol
> and the sound of your harps.
> Worms are spread out beneath you
> And your covering is worms."   (9–11)

The underworld is repellent; in the words of the author of Job 10, it is "a land of darkness and deep shadow" (26), "a land of darkness like gloom," "of deep shadow and confusion" (lit. of "no order," which the NRSV translates as "chaos") (22). There is no return, as Job mourns in 14:7. If only man were like a tree, capable of regeneration even from a buried root. If only death were a temporary purgatory (13–17).

> The cloud fades and departs
> So one who descends into Sheol will not rise
> He will no longer return to his home
> No longer will his domain acknowledge him.
>   (Job 7:9–10)

And yet certain threads in the tradition suggest that with the experience of death and under certain circumstances can come the peace granted by finality and eternal sleep.

We recall Samuel's complaint that Saul had "disturbed" him. In a motif typical of the lament genre, Job, who wishes he had died on the day of his birth rather than grow up to suffer, says, "For now I would be lying down and quiet / I would sleep; then I would be at rest . . ." (3:13). The sociological leveling of all who die is seen not as a final indignity, as implied in Isaiah 14, but as a relief (see Job 3:15–19). Prisoners finally have relief from their taskmasters and slaves from their lords. The great and the small lie together in a less negative eternal community.

And yet for the rest to be perfect, certain conditions must be met. Job 21:32 mentions the watch that the living are to keep over the tomb. There are dangers in the passage from life to death. Moreover, the good death means that one lies in one's own tomb, not thrown out from the grave "like loathsome carrion" (See NRSV: Isa. 14:19). Proper burial helps to ensure the peaceful death, as in many other traditional cultures.

Polemics within the Hebrew Bible and archaeological evidence suggest that Israelites propitiated their dead, regarding them as achieving in death some of the status of the divine immortals. Theodore Lewis has discussed in detail the various terms applied to the dead and to those who would consult them (1987:281). The dead are *'ĕlōhîm* or *'ēlîm* (lit. "gods") or *rĕpā'îm* ("shades"). Lewis suggests that Isaiah 57 polemizes against the pouring out of libations to the dead and the bringing of offerings (6). He interprets the text to mean that Israelites consulted their ancestors to obtain oracles (8). Israelites hope, falsely in the view of the author of the polemic, for the help, deliverance, and influence the ancestral spirits are believed to provide. Wealthy Israelites left in the burial caves of their departed the remainders of feasts for the dead, numerous libation bowls, lamps, and other evidence of possible ritual action (Mazar 1992:521–26). Sometimes the tombs contain material valuables such as the two small silver plaques, inscribed with versions of the priestly blessing of Numbers, left in the burial tomb of Ketef Hinnom. Are such offerings literally intended for the dead who may intercede with God or cause us harm, or are they gifts in memory of the deceased, a kind of memorial? Do those who leave flowers on the grave of an ancestor believe he or she propitiates them in some literal sense, or are the offerings evidence of our need to remember our departed friends and relatives and to honor them? Do we not still participate in cults for the dead?

Ps. 106:28 associates the eating of "sacrifices for the dead" with Moabite religion and the idolatrous worship of Baal Peor, while Deut. 26:14 is generally interpreted by scholars as a condemnation of making offerings to the dead, although the text is ambiguous (see Ackerman 1992:145; see also Bloch-Smith 1992:223). Is it forbidden to offer the sacred portion of produce, the tithe (see Deut. 26:13), to the dead or is it forbidden to make any sort of offering to the dead? Passages such as Isa. 8:19–20 and Deut. 18:11–12 also warn against attempts to raise the dead or consult them by means of spirit mediums, as do Lev. 19:26; 31 and 20:6, 27. On the other hand, some interpret the commandment to honor one's father and mother (Exod. 20:12, Deut. 5:16, and 27:16) as having to do with providing for one's ancestors after death (see Brichto 1973:30–31), a notion that archaeological evidence can be interpreted to support. And even the metaphoric image in Jer. 31:15 of Rachel weeping for her children and intervening on their behalf implies the continued involvement of ancestors in the lives of the living. Threads more and less sympathetic to cults of the ancestors are thus preserved in the Bible, although it is still not certain, despite comparative ancient Near Eastern evidence, what "offerings" meant in terms of worldview or what diviners did.

While the topic of life after death is a complex one in ancient Israelite religion, and while we will never fully comprehend the range of Israelite attitudes toward death or completely understand the implications of their ritual actions, it does seem certain that the Israelites believed that one descended to Sheol after death and was transformed.

The major transition in the mythology of the afterlife occurred in the late-biblical period, when some Israelites came to accept not merely the idea that after death one became a shade with some sort of material existence, but that the dead could actually come back to concrete life by means of resurrection.

Already in the literary form called the lament the metaphor of death and rebirth described the sufferer's hope for ultimate vindication. Though he be surrounded by the chords of death, drowning in a watery abyss, indeed, brought down to Sheol itself, he will be redeemed and given a second chance at life worth living. These images and themes are found in Job, in Isaiah 53 (the so-called psalm of the suffering servant), and in numerous hymns (Ps. 22:14–15, 17–18, 19–21 and 18:4–5, 16–19; Jon. 2:5–6). Death, watery chaos, earthly suffering and their reversal suggest the ancient mythic pattern found in the Canaanite story of Baal and Anat, where emptiness becomes fullness and the waste a fertile plain. In apocalyptic passages such as Isa. 25: 6–8, 26:19, and 27:1 the mythic pattern of creation and the popular metaphor of rebirth are projected onto expectations for a new day, a new time, a metahistorical reality that nevertheless can be actualized and experienced on earth. On that day Chaos will be conquered permanently, Leviathan will be killed (Isa. 27:1), and Sea's twin brother Death will be "swallowed up forever" (25:7). Note the banquet motif that accompanies the conquest of death (25:6). "Your dead will live and [their] corpses will rise. Wake up and rejoice, dwellers of the dust." "The earth will give birth to [lit. drop] the shades" (26:19) (see also Dan. 12:2). It is within this constellation of motifs that the first-century Paul understands the events surrounding Jesus. It is the same set of motifs that informs Jews about the world-to-come at some future time; and in this way in Judaism and Christianity myths of world creation intertwine with beliefs about human beings' capacity to be recreated, released from the chaos that is death.

Israelite mythology involving origins and death thus serves as an important response both to questions about individual existence and the life of the community. One of the ways in which Israelites tried to make sense of human mortality was by viewing life as the temporal, concrete, and best portion of a longer, supramundane timeline. One had only one "real" life to live and had to make the most of one's stay in God's created world. They made sense of the workaday existence by viewing it as the result of the first humans' errors in the garden. There is no need for guilt, but there is also no way to return to paradise for much of Israel's intellectual history. One must make the best of one's stay in the good world that God has created. The creation of the people Israel, the establishment of her major monarchic-period institutions, and Israelite hopes for renewal after the calamity of exile are all placed with the pattern of creation myth, the victory–enthronement. Indeed, the various uses of this pattern mirror Israel's social history: pre-monarchic, monarchic, and post-monarchic. And yet world creation in the opening chapters of Genesis omits the battle motif, the shapers of the tradition perhaps wishing in this case to set the Yahwistic Israelite tradition apart form those of neighboring cultures.

Myths of origin and myths of death are intertwined in the late-biblical tradition by authors who hope to pry open the closed gates of paradise. In the genre of apocalyptic, new creation comes to be synonymous with the defeat of Death, the ultimate Chaos. Not all Israelites in post-monarchic times shared this vision of a new world order, but the tradition provided the rich raw material, the building blocks, shared and recognized by all Israelites, that apocalypticists could adapt and perceive through their own eyes. These pieces of the tradition were combined and understood in divers ways that remained true and meaningful to various groups over the course of Israelite history and in the many threads that contribute to the tradition as it has come down to us.

SUGGESTED READINGS

For an excellent introduction to various theories of myth and a discussion of the multidisciplinary definitions of myth, see William Doty's *Mythography* (1986). Among Mircea Eliade's classic works on humans' attempts to grapple with their origins and their need to revisit those early days in myth and ritual, see, for example, *The Myth of the Eternal Return* (1965). Among the many collections of traditional narratives about the creation of the universe and its initial ordering, one should mention Sir James Frazier's methodologically dated but still useful *Folklore in the Old Testament* (1918) and Theodore Gaster's elaboration and transformation of this work. For a more recent collection, see Barbara C. Sproul's *Primal Myths* (1979). On the Israelite use of the victory–enthronement creation pattern, see Susan Niditch (1984), Richard J. Clifford, and Frank Moore Cross. For a translation of "Baal and Anat" and other Canaanite myths, see Coogan.

For an excellent recent study of Israelite views of death and the afterlife, as well as related ritual and mythic patterns see Theodore Lewis's *Cults of the Dead* (1989). By way of contrast, see Brian B. Schmidt's *Israel's Beneficent Dead* (1995).

For a fine overview of archaeological evidence in the light of biblical material, see Elizabeth Bloch-Smiths article "The Cult of the Dead in Judah" (1992).

On apocalyptic, see the bibliographic entries by Hanson, Collins, and Cook.

4

The Legal and Ethical Dimension

Law texts within the collection of traditional writings called the Hebrew Bible offer a special challenge as we seek to understand and
empathize with the Israelites who wrote down the laws and to relate
these seeming collections of legal dicta to actual ways of life, to living
cultures.

The texts are integrated into culture-shaping and culture-reflecting
narration—what God gave to Moses or spoke to him at specific sacred
locations in certain foundational situations, and what Moses told the
people. They are, moreover, both fragments and expansions. A collection such as Exodus 21–23 addresses only certain legal situations or
issues and is surely an incomplete sampling of Israel's customary case
law relevant to understanding the way of life in one or more periods
or settings. At the same time, the laws, once written down, became
artifacts to be redacted or elaborated. As elsewhere in the ancient Near
East, the codes were not meant to be complete but only representative,

a mere selection, and once written down they became frozen, set pieces, no longer living and changing in the community (see Oppenheim 1964: 158, 231–232; see also Goody 1968, 15). Such written codes, collected and inserted within the Hebrew Bible, may well reflect the worldview of the particular writers/redactors but not necessarily actual Israelite law customs. In many instances the texts reveal conceptions of the way the world should work.

Covenant

As was discussed in the chapter on the experiential dimension, Israel's relationship with God is described in Hebrew Scriptures as a covenant. The covenant is, in fact, rooted in a wider ancient Near Eastern political concept involving the relationship between lords and their vassals in a feudal form of government.

Over the years, archaeologists have unearthed numerous examples of ancient Near Eastern treaties characterized by a recurrent conventionalized format. First comes a preamble (e.g., the Hittite treaty dating from 1450–1200 B.C.E., translated in ANET:203–5, states: "These are the words of the Sun," the Hittite King . . .); there follows a history of the relationship between the treaty partners (information about the grandfather of this vassal, his rebellion, etc.); then follow stipulations regarding the relationship of the partners ("You be loyal to me. I will be loyal to you."); next there is an invocation to the gods as witnesses (e.g., the sun god); there is a provision for inscribing the treaty and placing it in a temple ("The words are inscribed on this tablet"); and finally there are blessings and curses ("If Duppi Tessub does not honor these words, may these gods destroy him . . ."). If one explores passages such as Exodus 20, Exodus 21–23, Joshua 24, large sections of Deuteronomy, and key concepts lying behind the oracles of the biblical prophets, one begins to understand the pervasiveness of the notion of covenant as a means of describing God's relationship with Israel. Implicitly one begins to discover what a wide range of biblical writers considered to be proper ethical behavior.

In this way, the Ten Commandments of Exodus 20 might be viewed as an abbreviated version of a treaty form. The opening verse serves as a brief preamble and historical prologue. Lord Yahweh identifies himself as the one who brought Israel out of Egypt (lit. from the "house" of slaves). Nuances of blessing and cursing are found in verses 5 and 6 and in the commandment to honor one's parents. Other aspects of the treaty form are more fully represented in Joshua 24 and Deuteronomy (e.g., the naming of witnesses, the provision for deposit). The dominant portion of Exodus 20 consists of a set of stipulations or rules of behavior required of Israel as treaty partner.

The Ten Commandments

In brief, Exodus 20 points to the way human beings are to relate to one another and to God. The code can roughly be divided into halves. The commandments in 20:1–7 all have to do with the way human beings are to think of and relate to Yahweh. Strongly Yahwist and iconoclastic, these verses express some of the threads in worldview that dominate the Hebrew Bible: God is the rescuer who brought Israel out of slavery in Egypt; no gods beside Yahweh are to be worshiped and Israel is to make no images or icons that become the locus for obeisance; God's name is not to be used inappropriately, especially in false vows. As we know from biblical polemics and the extrabiblical evidence discussed in chapter 1, not all Israelites in ancient times shared these views, but they have come to shape Judaism.

In the context of God's jealousy and indictments of polytheism and iconism, there appears a troubling message about the nature of God's punishment and approval. God punishes children for the iniquity of parents to the third and fourth generation of those who hate God but shows steadfast love to the thousandth generation of those who love God by keeping his commandments. It is clear from a proverb quoted in Jeremiah (31:29) and Ezekiel (18:2) that it was a common belief that the children suffer for the sins of the parents: "The parents eat unripened grapes, but the children's teeth are blunted." One thinks of the curse besetting the family of Oedipus. Beliefs in family curses or blessings—here theologically specified as punishment or reward for covenant faithfulness or lack thereof—are the ways in which many groups of human beings have attempted to explain undeserved suffering. The Deuteronomistic writer explains the untimely death of his hero-king Josiah as punishment for the sins of Josiah's grandfather, Menasseh (2 Kings 23:26). Job's friends, moreover, use the sin of previous generations to explain that good man's suffering. Indeed, Jeremiah and Ezekiel both quote the proverb about the sour grapes in order to suggest that in a future ideal time the proverb will no longer apply—as if to hope for a renewed paradise that will correct the truth of the proverbial wisdom ingrained in the relationship with God. A critique of this thread in the inherited theology is implied in certain texts, but the concept of inherited blessing or punishment is considered important or representative enough to have been included in the brief code of Exodus 20. Is the statement at Exod. 20:5–6 hyperbolic, insisting that God's blessings for keeping the covenant are so great that they long outlast one's lifetime, showering down continued blessings upon descendants, and outlasting the results of the evil that people do? Will the continuing blessing from the good ancestor always overshadow the punishment from the one who is not faithful to God?

The centerpiece of the little code in Exodus 20 involves the Sabbath, an important demarcator of the week's experience that invokes the closure of the creation process. Israelites are required to encode the rhythm of their weeks with the pattern of Yahweh's work as world creator. The Sabbath thus becomes an important symbolic link between the divine/human relationship and the human way of life, which is further addressed in verses 12–17.

At the head of the laws in verses 12–17 is the command to honor one's mother and father. Some scholars suggest that this verse originally referred to a cult of the dead, requiring the children to pay proper ritual attention to those buried in family tombs. (See chaps. 1 and 2 for a fuller discussion of this thread in ancient Israelite religion.) Such attitudes toward the dead, involving notions of the need for their propitiation and of their continued presence among and influence upon the living, appear to be deeply rooted in the religion of Israel, as discussed in the chapter on myth. This concept was rejected and subsumed under the rubric of superstition by other voices in the tradition, in particular those responsible for the current form of Deuteronomy, a work that includes the "ten commandments" as a central periocope (Deuteronomy 5). Hence the Greek name for the book, meaning "second law." For such readers of or listeners to the commandments whose views have shaped our own understanding of Scripture as Jews or Christians, the law concerning parents emphasizes honor for the living ancestors. Implicit is the importance of the nuclear family as a microcosm of the larger society and as a human-to-human echo of the relationship between the deity and humans. The nuclear family is emphasized in the creation myth of Genesis (2:24) as a feature of the world order that was meant to be. Care for one's parents guarantees long life, a specific promise made for none of the other commandments. In a world without security in which families may exist at a bare subsistence level, generations of kin are a source of political and economic protection and survival. The care for kin (the closer the kin, the greater the obligation to care) is integral to Israelite worldview. Indeed, the Jacobite genealogy that came to express Israel's concept of the people mythologically forges family ties among once disparate groups. It is hoped that such bonds secure honor among kin. Providing a foundation for all such honor are the biologically and psychologically rooted mutual obligations of parents and children.

While societies define murder or stealing differently, all societies have some sort of rules that govern the taking of life or property and prohibit illicit killing or stealing. The term for taking life in verse 13 is *rāṣaḥ* "murder," not the more general "to kill". In androcentric Israel, the commission of adultery is to be understood as stealing, as the command ordering one not to covet indicates. "You shall not covet your neighbor's house; you shall not covet your neighbor's wife . . . or ox . . . or anything that belongs to your neighbor" (17). To commit adultery is to steal another man's wife or the wife's allowing herself to be taken; it is not defined as a man being unfaithful to his wife. Bearing false witness, especially in capital cases, is a form of murder; in more minor accusations it is nevertheless an act of unwarranted aggression that leads to the abuse of the innocent. Like the command to honor parents, laws against murder, stealing, adultery, and bearing false witness all have to do with strengthening and ordering society.

In a sense, the cosmogonic process continues with the setting of general rules for behavior among people. The commandments not to covet are an important part of world-ordering. Whereas people can observe or uncover breaches of covenant described in Exod. 20:12–16, coveting may be a matter of internal thought, accessible only to God. And yet desiring what belongs to one's neighbor can be as destructive of society as actual stealing. The emphasis on one's thoughts also serves as a reminder that deep within the Israelite tradition is a concern with motivation and the internal, psychological dynamic of religious belief. You are not only what you do but also how you feel and what you contemplate doing. Recall the interesting description of the generation of the flood, that the very framing of the thoughts of their hearts was evil all the time. (Gen. 6:5) That is, the very work of their imagination was up to no good. Similarly, the tale of Cain's murder of his brother Abel pictures sin as a crouching demon lying in wait to tempt the mind of Cain (Gen. 4: 7).

The Ten Commandments are a brief statement of the ethical obligations of an Israelite that became an important template or guide within the tradition cited twice in full in Exodus and Deuteronomy. The commandments bind Israel to God with covenantal stipulations that define the nature of Yahwism in accordance with the dominant biblical message of Yahweh-alonism and aniconism. Central to this notion of Yahwism is the weekly ritual return to God's creation through the cessation of work on the seventh day. Finally, Exodus 20 lays out essential ground rules for human interaction.

In its current form, the Ten Commandments articulate a particular Israelite worldview, the one perhaps most recognizable to modern readers that comes to dominate the written, preserved version of the tradition. The Yahweh alonism is probably at least as old as early conservative Levitical circles such as those represented by the ninth-century northern prophets Elijah and Elisha. The central place of the Sabbath may be a late-biblical emphasis, one that becomes a key definer of Judaism. The command to honor parents (whatever the connotation) and laws against murder, adultery, stealing, bearing false witness, and coveting could be as old as Israel itself, being possible foundations for any group.

In seeking to understand the worldviews of the ancient Israelites more precisely, however, we need to ask how such general rules were specified and how, if at all, they were to be enforced.

Case Law

In the case of the Sabbath, for example, what constitutes work? Can one do recreational but tiring activity? If one is a physician, can one practice one's healing arts? Can one treat only a life-threatening emergency? Is stealing a loaf of bread when you are starving the same as stealing one when you are full? Is stealing bread the same as stealing precious jewels? While the postbiblical Rabbis deal with many of these questions within their own concepts of order and system—concepts which for modern readers do not necessarily tally with our notions of completeness or systemization—the legal material preserved in the rest of the Hebrew Bible does not systematically take up the general rules in Exodus 20 and "fill them out" in order to apply them to daily life.

Nevertheless, Exod. 21:1–22:17, the first half of the so-called Covenant Code in Exodus 21–23 is a selective body of civil and criminal case law that does go beyond the sort of grand and simple statements and commands found in Exod. 20:2–17. The very format of the material in Exodus 21–22 sets up casuistic settings. "When . . . (21:28), "If . . ." (21:30), "Whoever . . ." (21:16, 17), "But if . . ." (21:5).

> If someone's ox hurts the ox of his neighbor and it dies, they will sell the live ox and divide its price, and also the dead one they will divide. But if it is known that it has a history of being a goring ox and its owner did not take care about it, he shall fully recompense an ox for an ox, but the dead ox is for him. (Exod. 21:35–36)

The Covenant Code in Exodus shares some essentials with other ancient Near Eastern and modern law codes, such as the possibility of monetary compensation (Exod. 21:18–19; 22:6–7 [Hebrew: 22:5–6]; 21:22; 21:33–35; 22:1–4 [Hebrew 21:37–22: 3] cf. Code of Hammurabi, ANET 163–80, 1.209]). The Covenant Code also offers the modern reader many surprises, revealing the writer's assumptions about the workings of society and the individual's obligations under the law.

The Israelites practiced slavery (21:6–7, 26–27, 20) and the writer is able to calculate human worth in financial terms. The Bible asserts that the firstborn of humans and animals is the Lord's, a most valuable offering, a precious commodity (Exod. 13:12–13; 34:19–20; Num. 3: 41, 45). Whereas such passages are generally accompanied by a rejoinder concerning the ransoming of the first born, Exod. 22:29 [Hebrew 22:28] declares more simply and starkly, "The firstborn of your sons you shall give to me." This statement, placed between commandments concerning offerings from the fields and animal resources, seems to support the notion that child sacrifice was indeed a thread in ancient Israelite religion.

Women's lives are circumscribed in men's terms: a man may sell his daughter as a slave (21:7); a man who seduces a virgin lowers her economic worth to her father, who must be compensated (22:16 [Hebrew 22:15]). Women also have certain rights under this system (see 21:7ff.). The man may have more than one wife (the woman must be monogamous), but if he takes a second wife he must not diminish the food, clothing, or conjugal rights (which some translate as "housing") of the first wife (Exod. 21:10).

Most ethically appealing in the code is the concern enjoined for widows, orphans, and resident aliens. The latter are a legal category of people from a non-Israelite state who are allowed to reside in Israel. Like widows and orphans, foreigners are marginal figures of society (22:21–24 [Hebrew 22:20–23]). God is perceived as the appeal court for and the champion of such victims; the punishment for the oppressor, as in many other cases of wrongdoing in the Covenant Code, is *lex talionis* ("an eye for an eye"). Note the parallel traditional style of the lines.

> If indeed you oppress them
> When they cry out to me with force
> I will surely hear their cry.
> (22:21 [Hebrew 22:22]

My wrath will burn
I will kill you with the sword
Your wives will be widows
Your children orphans.
(22:22 [Hebrew 22:23])

Such law codes reveal much about their framers' sense of social relations. They project a society in which some are economically better off than others, but those who are better off are required to adhere to certain tenets of economic justice (22:25–27 [Hebrew 22:24–26]; (see later discussion on Deuteronomy). Those who are capable of lending money cannot charge interest from fellow Israelites (22:25 [Hebrew 22:24]. It is interesting that some sort of cash economy is envisioned as operative, and the use of objects as collateral is also present. If a poor person pawns his cloak, it is to be returned to him before sundown. If he shivers due to the cold of the night and cries out to God, God will listen. God speaks in this code—it is, after all, framed as an instruction to Moses from God—and describes himself as "compassionate" (22:27 [Hebrew 22:26]) to members of the underclass.

The social world implied by this code has no tightly centralized authority to enforce it. There is no reference to a monarchy at all, only to a "leader of your people" (22:28 [Hebrew 22:27]), which may refer to some sort of tribal or clan chieftain. Exod. 23:7–8 appears to be addressed to officials of some sort, perhaps local judges or elders. Reference is also made to "being brought before God" (22:8 [Hebrew 22:7]), seeking an oracle at a shrine. To decide a dispute, one party may also take an oath before God, an action deemed so serious and taken so soberly that the other disputant must accept what the party who swears by God declares to be true (22:11 [Hebrew 22:10]). Whether or not oracles or oaths actually restored the balance in cases where the body politic had been disturbed is uncertain, but the code creates an image of a society without complicated bureaucratic legal strategies to establish or reestablish order.

Indeed, the law is taken into one's own hands as regards defending or revenging kin. (Exod. 21:13; cf. Num. 35:19, 21). The parent has the power of life and death over his children (21:15, 17). As in the Ten Commandments, respect for parents underlies society.

Individuals are charged with the responsibility for fairness and honesty, a prerequisite for any stable society. One must bear honest witness and have the moral autonomy to speak the truth even if the majority lies, nor can one allow sympathy for the poor to influence one's judgment (23:3) or antipathy to prevent one from doing the right thing when the "enemy" needs one's help (23:5).

In setting the authors of this code in a specific social and historical context, one notes that many of the issues raised in the code and the examples provided have to do with an agrarian and pastoral life: standing grain that catches fire; goring oxen; stolen sheep; trampled vineyards. Ownership of oxen, donkeys, and sheep dominate the code.

Given its interests and point of view, the Covenant Code may well predate the monarchy. The agrarian and pastoral highland culture, with its decentralized political structure, well suits the code. Of course, it must be admitted that this culture continued in some form throughout the history of Israel. One wonders how much the existence of the central government, northern or southern, affected the farmers' day-to-day lives. To be sure, taxes, conscription, potential visits by court officials, and the nearby presence of military installations could all affect worldview, but the passage of the seasons and the power of the elders in an androcentric, patrilineal system, worries about livestock and olive presses, and concerns of family and kin would remain strong even once the highland culture was supplanted or better supplemented with a more urban culture during the monarchy.

Law in Deuteronomy

The biblical law codes are sets of soundings from various segments of Israelite society, possibly describing worlds of different periods and purview. It is interesting to turn to Deuteronomy and see how its framers deal with many of the same issues discussed in the Covenant Code of Exodus or in the Ten Commandments. There is some overlap: the importance of respect for parents; the command to worship only Yahweh; and concern for honesty in legal transactions. Deuteronomy, in fact, includes a version of the Ten Commandments. Note the grounding of the Sabbath in the exodus and in remembrance of God's deliverance (5:15) rather than in world creation as in Exodus 20. People creation is the primary founding myth. Deuteronomy includes other fascinating departures and nuances that reveal much about a particular thread in Israelite culture.

Deuteronomy functions within the larger biblical story as a testament of the leader Moses, his wise words of advice and his review of key events in his life and the life of the people before he dies. The style of Deuteronomy is appropriately homiletical, many of Moses' speeches being rich in the use of rhetorical questions, second-person address, and cohortatives. The framework of Deuteronomy is strongly covenantal, the message of blessing for the faithful and curses for the unfaithful being quintessentially Deuteronomic.

What is Torah faithfulness in this work? As in the Covenant Code, one dimension of the sampling of law in this work deals with matters of economic justice. As in Exodus 21–23, it is assumed that there will always be economically disadvantaged members of the community (Deut. 15:7–11, esp. v. 11). Concern is expressed for widows and orphans (10:17–18). The Deuteronomic Code also includes instructions providing for Levites (14:27, 28–29; 18:1–8). It is assumed that the Levites (the tribe to which Moses and Aaron belong) do not have ancestral agricultural holdings in specific geographic locations (though certain cities are described as being theirs), but that members of the group serve throughout Israel as teachers, singers, priests and in a variety of other important culture sustaining functions (see 27: 14). While it is not possible to explore fully the complex and difficult-to-reconstruct history of the Levites in the northern and southern kingdoms, Deuteronomy's sympathetic and supportive attitude to Levites seems to point to Levitical origins of the work. Particularly in the southern monarchy, where centralization of worship became an important political goal, the Levites may have found themselves virtually unemployed since many of their functions were cultic and shrine-related. The tithe or tenth taken from agricultural products and livestock would serve not only to maintain communal feasts and festivals (14:22–26) but also serve as a foodbank for the Levites, who were listed along with widows, orphans, and resident aliens as being among the marginal in this culture (28–29).

The most dramatic example of Deuteronomy's code of economic ethics has to do with the sabbatical (Deut. 15:1–18). The tradition of giving the land a "sabbath," or rest, by leaving it fallow in the seventh year may well be an ancient Israelite custom (see Exod. 23:10–11). The sabbatical also came to be associated with the freeing of slaves (Exod. 21:2–11). Deuteronomy broadens the manumission to include male and female slaves and narrows it to Israelites ("a member of your community") rather than to "Hebrew slaves." Originally, in the language of ancient Israel the word "Hebrew" may well have applied to marginal, stateless folk, a class rather than an ethnic group, and this understanding of "Hebrew" may apply at Exod. 21:2–11. Most radical in Deuteronomy is the forgiveness of debts that now also applies to Israelite debtors in the seventh year. Notice the way the homilist, in the voice of Moses, talks to his listeners. Those who are well enough off to provide loans and those who may need them are addressed; the latter are allowed to recognize their right to borrow under the law, as envisioned by the author.

> If there is a poor person
> from among your brethren
> within one of your gates
> in your land
> which the Lord your God is giving you,
> do not harden your heart
> or shut your hand
> from your poor brother.
> You will surely open your hand to
> him. . . .
>   (Deut. 15:7–8)

Loans are to be adequate for the borrower's needs; interest is not to be charged to fellow Israelites (23:19), nor is an approaching sabbatical to become a cause for not lending for fear that soon all debts will be forgiven (15:9). It is to be recognized and accepted that any loan to a fellow Israelite may become an outright grant. On some level the

author envisions a kind of modified utopia in which all have some
access to the riches of the community. They may not be wealthy, but
a secure safety net is provided. The poor are to be shown respect (24:
13), paid on time for work done and on a daily basis (24:14). Respect
for persons is also expressed in the commandment not to return es-
caped slaves (23:15), a potentially subversive law that challenges more
typical ancient Near Eastern custom, in permission granted the individual to eat grapes in a neighbor's vineyard or to pluck some ears of
corn to relieve immediate hunger (23:24–25; cf. the more limited pro-
visions in Exod. 23:10–11), and in the requirement that landowners
leave some of their remaining produce unharvested in the trees or on
the land so that it be readily available to the widow, the orphan, and
the alien—the marginals in Israelite society (24:19–21)—a law also
found in Lev. 19:9–10 and 23:22.

All such injunctions come with reminders that you were a slave in
Egypt (24: 22, 18). Israel's founding myth is thus a basis for identification with the weakest in society. Israelites need to retain sympathy
for the poor since God had mercy upon them. Mythology and economic law intertwine. It is in the light of this image of community
justice that Deuteronomy's strong message about blessing and cursing
makes sense. The contrast between fertility, peace, and well-being for
the good and sterility, war, and deprivation for the evil so strongly
emphasized in Deuteronomy refers less to each person's morality than
to the tenor of a society. Are the poor cared for? Is God respected?
Are the leaders honest? While society is made up of individuals, and
while individual choices affect the community as a whole, the issue
in Deuteronomy is articulated differently than in Job, which focuses
on the innocence or guilt of one man. What sort of community are
you?

Community in Deuteronomy

Deuteronomy offers a very circumscribed image of the community;
the group is defined in strict Yahwistic terms, in accordance with its
authors' own concept of God's people. "Us" and "them" are clearly
defined. "Them" is frequently non-Israelite and is revealed in the way

the authors present rules for warring and the treatment of enemies. This interest is part and parcel of the work's narrative function in the larger Israelite myth. Deuteronomy reviews Israel's previous encounters with enemies and prepares for the conquest to come, but the theme of war also provides an opportunity to define the group over against the other. For those who share the worldview of Deuteronomy, the enemy is also within.

Enemies Without

War-code material is found in Deuteronomy 20, 21:10–14, and 23:9–14. Chapter 20 provides a set format for the way in which one proceeds to war. A prewar ritual emphasizes the need for Israel's fighting force to be of a pure, totally focused frame of mind (1–9). The priest has a homiletical role, as do the officials, and finally the commanders take charge of the group, which has been cleansed of the faint-hearted or those who may have their minds on other matters. The battle scene provides a microcosm of Israelite leadership in the Deuteronomic view, with priestly, secular, and military authorities.

As Johannes Pedersen, Mary Douglas, and Norman Gottwald have noted from different perspectives, the authors' concern is with wholeness and neatness. The small, committed fighting force, holy and whole, can succeed. The sensitivity to the psychology of the fighters is marked. The concern with purity and wholeness emerges in a more physical fashion at 23:9–14. The warriors' camp is to be kept in a state of ritual purity, uncontaminated by sources of human uncleanness. War is ritual, the warrior an acolyte. Again the priestly or Levitical quality of Deuteronomic worldview is clear.

Deut. 20:10–20 and 21:10–14 provide a sort of warrior's code for wars of aggression. Destruction is somewhat limited to certain groups and circumstances, food-bearing trees are protected, and parameters are set forth for the treatment of captive women.

In fact, Deut. 20:10–18 attempts to accommodate two war ideologies, one aggressive but pragmatic, in which enemies are offered a chance to trade their freedom for their lives, and the other involving the total annihilation of "the ban," whereby nothing that breathes is allowed to live. The enemy is a cancer, a potentially bad influence that could sully a pure Israel. They must be rooted out lest their bad influence tempt Israel to sin (18). The violence is thus justified. The author of Deuteronomy 20 harmonizes these two war ideologies by asserting that the former is for faraway towns, the latter for the people who live within Israel's promised inheritance. In the larger biblical tradition, these neat boundaries for warring behavior are not maintained.

Indeed, for the whole of chapter 20, as for much of the book, the authors of Deuteronomy schematize and idealize, creating a model for society, a planned theocracy rather than reflecting an actual world.

Enemies Within

In this purified, pristine whole that is the utopia of the Deuteronomic writers, all those who worship other gods or "entice" others to worship them are to be executed. The ban can be turned against a whole Israelite city should worship of other gods take place there (13:12–18 [Hebrew 13:13–19]). Even the possessions of those executed by the sword are to be destroyed and the town reduced to rubble, for disloyalty to Yahweh is a veritable contagious disease that must be eliminated by fire (17 [Hebrew 13:18]). It is most extensively and specifically in the law code of Deuteronomy that one finds prohibitions and condemnations of some of the activities and religious symbols that the archaeological record and ethnographic reconstructions suggest were common in Israelite religion. The use of "asheras" and "standing stones" next to Yahweh's altar, perhaps symbolizing of the indwelling presence of the deity and his consort (see the earlier discussion of Kuntillet ʿAjrud), is prohibited (Deut. 16:21–22). Child sacrifice is condemned (18:10), as is the practice of consulting the dead, with its implied beliefs about the underworld and life after death (11). The Deuteronomic writers clearly lay out what they consider proper Yahwism and thereby draw a distinction between the "true" and "false" Israel, between religion and magic, between us and them.

The notion of Israel as a whole, cleansed and uniform in values and in its religious and ethical life, a world in which definition is clear, in which things are black and white also extends to the assorted rules in

Deut. 22:4–12. Like comparable material in Lev. 19:19, these laws view the world in terms of distinct categories that no human being may artificially blur. Women may not wear men's clothing, nor men women's clothing (5). Only one sort of seed may be sowed in a vineyard (9). One may not plow with an ox and donkey yoked together (10), nor wear clothes made of linen and wool woven together (11). The Deuteronomists, like their levitical counterparts in Leviticus 19, view God's created world as containing boundaries never to be crossed or confused. They uphold as well the distinctions between food edibles and unclean edibles that are nonfood to Israelites (Deuteronomy 14). (The various categories of food will be discussed in more detail when exploring the priestly holiness code of Leviticus.) Along with other priestly writers whose views on food and sex come to dominate classical expressions of Judaism, the authors of Deuteronomy seek to avoid that which is betwixt and between categories as defined and thereby to keep the cosmos intact and chaos at bay.

All cultures create categories of some sort. Who among us would feel comfortable eating a witchetty grub? In contrast to aboriginal Australians, to us a grub is not considered food. In wearing underwear on the outside or in purposely making themselves up to resemble the opposite gender, pop figures such as Madonna or Boy George test and challenge the neat categories that make us comfortable and through which most of us define ourselves. We are often as intolerant of category blurrers as were the biblical writers, or perhaps our culture has been strongly shaped by theirs in ways we no longer recognize. During holidays such as Halloween or Mardi Gras we, in fact, institutionalize or permit such reversals and disguises of usual categories, if only to reinforce the workaday ones or to offer us a temporary escape from their constraints, a rebellion against the comfortable status quo. In exploring the ritual dimension, it will be interesting to see if the Israelites provide for such allowable challenges to the categories of the comfortable.

The Deuteronomic writers define order in what some might regard as a particularly rigid fashion. The don't-let-the-peas-touch-the-potatoes mentality, together with the strict delineation between Yahwism and idolatry, with no gray areas in between, may reveal an Israelite community that is beset and oppressed, one that is less than assured about its own identity and security. It could be argued that such a group, insecure in its own self-definition, turns to increasingly stricter means of describing the true Israel. Chaos threatens and the immediate and controllable cosmos must be shored up.

Some of the laws in Deuteronomy are not unique to it or to a priestly orientation. In particular, laws pertaining to the family suit Israelite traditional social structure.

Family Ethics and Women

As in Exod. 21:15, the parents have the power of life and death over the child, who is deemed to be rebellious, an incorrigible "glutton and drunkard" (Deut. 21:18–21). Note, however, that true to their own special perspective, the Deuteronomic writers view dealing with such a son as a matter of literally "burning out the evil from your midst" (21). Again the message is to purify the community which should be uniform and whole. Upholding a patrilineal status quo, Deuteronomy strongly supports a law of male primogeniture (15–17), in contrast to the more serendipitous narrative traditions of Genesis, where the folktale pattern supersedes mundane custom so that the youngest succeeds. Another feature of the patrilineal, male-dominated system is the emphasis placed on the woman's virginity before marriage and upon her monogamy after marriage. The lines of male descent must be kept pure and unconfused. Woman provides the pure ground in which the man's offspring grow. Adulterous women and young, never-married women found not to be virgins at the time of their marriage are to be stoned, another instance of evil to be purged from the midst of the pure community (22:21, 22). In a visceral imaging of an obsession with male powers of reproduction, the writers declare that a woman who grabs a man's testicles during a heated argument between him and her husband is to have her hand cut off! (25:11–12)

The system envisioned by Deuteronomy provides certain rights or protections for women, all within the contours of an androcentric system in which young women are valuable exchange items, vital to the functioning and preservation of the group but commodities nevertheless. Deut. 22:13–19 describes a woman falsely accused of not being a virgin at the time of her marriage; v. 25 describes punishment by death for a man who rapes a woman in open territory, where no one can rescue her; and v. 28 deals with the rape of a virgin. In each case the matter is dealt with from society's androcentric perspective. In the first and last cases, recompense is offered the father of the girl for a devaluing of her worth, and the man must marry or stay married to her. The socio-structurally fuzzy prospect of an unmarried, less valuable daughter not properly married but no longer a virgin is apparently more troubling to those who partake of Deuteronomic (and a wider biblical) worldview than the notion of the young woman having to stay married to a man who detests and slanders her, or having to marry her rapist. That these situations might also disrupt social structure is not dealt with in the perspective of Deuteronomy. When a man is executed for rape, the punishment is meted out not because he raped a woman but because he sullied a woman legally bound to another man (24–25). Such attitudes toward and treatment of women are quite typical of traditional cultures and, like attitudes toward enemies in war, are to be understood within the context of a particular worldview.

Political Ethics

Some comments should be made concerning government as viewed by the Deuteronomic authors. Judges and officials are mentioned as being appointed "in all your towns" (lit. "gates," the sign of the urban location, the place where officials meet for judgment [16:18]). Notice how Israelites are homiletically addressed in 16:19, 20 not to pervert justice. The language is poetically parallelistic in the second person to produce a sermonizing style.

In contrast to the Covenant Code of Exodus, Deuteronomy does assume that the political landscape includes kings, but in contrast to other threads in Scripture that celebrate kingship and kings as divinely appointed heroes, Deuteronomy describes them as necessary evils whose inevitable tendency to excess has to be controlled. The king is not allowed to multiply horses or women, nor to acquire too much wealth for himself. He is to carry a copy of this law (probably the law pertaining to kings) upon his person, an amulet, written down by him (or for him) in the presence of the Levitical priests, to be read by him always so that he is reminded of his status as one member of God's holy community required to uphold God's law (see 17:14–20). The writers, familiar with kingship and its potential evils, imagine a king who must be controlled by the law and its Levitical teachers.

The Context

While the values and worldview found in the law of Deuteronomy could well extend back to conservative northern Levitical circles of an early monarchic date, they remain relevant in the traumas of northern conquest by Assyria in the eighth century B.C.E. and conquest of the southern kingdom by Babylonia in the sixth, for Israel's breaking of God's covenant as carefully defined in Deuteronomy, explains all of her political problems. Israel is being punished, suffering the covenantal curses described in Deuteronomy. The Deuteronomic writers not only explain Israel's contemporary situation but lay the groundwork for a hoped for, newly cleansed, and improved society along the lines of Deuteronomic Yahwism. The Deuteronomic vision of Israelite religion comes to dominate in the Hebrew Bible and in the religious traditions derived from ancient Israel that continue beyond biblical times.

Priestly Codes in Leviticus

In studying the legal and ethical dimension of Deuteronomy, we have already been introduced to key aspects of the priestly worldviews represented in Leviticus and Numbers (e.g., the overt and central concern with categories and avoiding confusion between them, and the essentially male perspective on cosmogony). Human societies frequently symbolize views of order in rules governing the body: definitions of foods one may eat and not eat, allowable and nonallowable sexual interaction, and customs governing interaction with the bodies of those who have died. The authors of Leviticus see the world in terms of "clean" and "unclean." The actual body, like Deuteronomy's body politic, is a vessel, a temple that must be properly maintained and kept pure, in order that the covenant with Yahweh be upheld and the life-preserving mediation between divine and human realms proceed. Chaos threatens in the form of death, illness, and various uncontrollable forces either real or imagined. The existence of definable categories for what sometimes seem to be mundane things and behavior is, in fact, meant to control the controllable, thereby creating a patina of order that makes the larger unknown chaos bearable.

For Israelites, the unclean becomes a metaphor for sin, so that one's behavior toward others and one's relationship with God also can be clean or unclean, producing the bounty of cosmos or the desolation of chaos. The creation myths explored in ch. 3 are thus interwoven into the essential fabric of God's covenantal relationship with Israel. The cosmogony is on-going and every Israelite is required to combat chaos and symbolically to represent the order of cosmos in his or her daily activity. The responsibility for upholding cosmos is especially incumbent upon priests, who perform the role of mediator in ritual. For them the wholeness and cleanness of the body is especially important. If they are unclean, they cannot serve in ritual. Their offerings, which may provide for atonement or seek well-being, will not be accepted by God. Thus, certain rules (e.g., those governing contact with the dead) apply only to them (compare Lev. 21:1–5, 11 and Num. 5:1–4; 19:11–22), but for a wide array of laws governing food and sexual contact, all Israelites are regarded as a nation of priests holy to God (Exod. 19:6).

Clean and Unclean

The section on clean and unclean foods in Leviticus 11 provides a good window on the nature of uncleanness and the way in which categories help to make sense of a culture. For a host of ecological, sociological, and historical reasons, Israelites defined edible animals to be of certain kinds. The edible mammals for example are those that have divided hooves and chew their cud. Thus, the pig that has divided hooves but does not chew its cud is ineligible as food; it falls between proper and accepted categories. Fish are to look like fish, having fins and scales, but all manner of eels or shellfish are inedible and unclean (see Douglas 1966). Uncleanness itself exudes from these forbidden foods, as well as from other cultural items deemed unclean according to the priestly system. It contaminates like an invisible poison; in this culture uncleanness is real and visceral, much like contagious bacteria and viruses, moving like a dangerous humour.

For example, Lev. 11:29 describes a host of "swarming creatures" that are unclean; these include the weasel, the mouse, the great lizard, and the gecko.

> And anything that one of them falls upon when they are dead becomes
>   unclean.
> Whether a wooden article or cloth, skin or sacking,
> any article that one does work with,
> it needs to be dipped in water
> and is unclean until evening
> and then it becomes clean.   (11:32)

Water purifies in the priestly code, as does the passage of the day. As the day turns to darkness, the status of the dipped object is renewed.

Rules governing sexual contact and bodily emissions are also interesting in terms of clean and unclean, chaos versus cosmos (see Lev. 12; 15). The man is rendered unclean after an emission of semen or after a discharge from illness, while the woman is unclean after a discharge of blood when the bleeding is irregular, during her monthly period, or in bleeding after giving birth. Various emissions convey somewhat different degrees of uncleanness and require various lengths of time and/or actions for the passage from unclean to clean status to be achieved. Again the uncleanness is visceral and contagious. A man with a discharge, a woman who has her period, and one who has vaginal bleeding that is not due to menstruation are unclean for seven days. Everything upon which they lie or sit becomes unclean, and anyone who comes into contact with that bed or seat must wash his clothes, bathe in water, and be unclean until evening. A man who has intercourse with an unclean woman himself conveys uncleanness to what he lies or sits upon.

Why should such emissions be considered unclean rendering? One scholar has suggested that since the body becomes a symbol for the ordered and defined whole of the cosmos, any seepage from its boundaries is considered anomalous and as rendering unclean. Yet the priests do not seek to contain tears or runny noses as sources of uncleanness. Nor is the concern merely with blood. An emission of semen renders one unclean, but blood shed during a murder is not considered as rendering unclean (cf. Num. 31:19 on blood and death on the battlefield; but even in Numbers the issue is not blood, but death).

It does seem that human sexual contact and the physical loci of that contact were regarded with special concern for order in this thread of the tradition. Sex has to do with passion and unruly human emotions, while the procreative results of the sex act place humans in the position of world creation itself—a heady notion. Thus men's sexuality is treated with caution and the need for definition; after an emission of semen, the man must be cleansed and renewed, while the woman who houses the very process whereby new humans are created is bounded, unclean monthly, in a continual passage from clean to unclean to clean, her cycles of fertility being a microcosm of the larger cyclical passages of the cosmos from chaos to order.

A practical result of woman's place in this pattern is her debarring— at least in the priestly codes preserved in the Bible—from public priestly leadership roles. That other threads in the tradition allowed for women priests is possible and perhaps even probable, as indicated by the lengths to which the author of the tale about Miriam in Numbers 12 goes to discredit the sister Levite of Moses and Aaron.

Another example of the way in which priestly authors seek to carve order out of daily experience is found in the laws governing prohibited marriages in Leviticus 18. All traditional societies attempt to steer a middle course between marriage too far outside the group and marriage that is too close within the group. On the one hand, foreigners are to be distrusted as not "us"; on the other hand, marriage to certain relatives may be regarded as incestuous, too much "us," confusing mothers with wives or brothers with husbands and infringing upon other categories in the system. What is perhaps most interesting about Leviticus 18 is that, like uncleanness, family status is contagious, so that one is prohibited from sexual relations not only with various blood relatives (see 7, 9, 10, 11, 12, 13) but also with a variety of affines (see e.g., 18:17, 18) or those with whom one's kin have had conjugal relationships (e.g., the widowed wife of your father's brother [14], or your brother's widow [16]). The marriage laws like those concerning foods are not proof of an ancient practical knowledge of science concerning the dangers of contaminated pig flesh or the medical risks of too small a gene pool. Rather, Israelites developed a system of conjugal categories that order their world, and the system addresses in-marrying as well as genetic relations. It is also of interest that the narratives of Genesis contradict some of these laws. For example, Jacob marries two sisters. It may well be that not all Israelites shared all the priestly categories or participated fully in that system, or that over time priestly rules were accepted by a larger community—all of which brings us to questions of provenance and dating.

There were undoubtedly priestly groups in Israel from the earliest pre-monarchic times serving at the various cultic centers explored by archaeologists and frequently mentioned in the Hebrew Bible. Such members of the community may well have been keepers of the sort of dietary and sexual customs later preserved in written form, but it is not possible to know how general in the population and how early were the priestly concepts of cleanness and uncleanness, order and chaos, concepts that come to dominate in postbiblical Judaism. The priestly voice in the final form of the collection we call the Hebrew Bible is very strong and presents its system of self-definition as definitive and as old as mythic times themselves.

The Prophets, the Covenant, and Purity

The prophetic corpus covers a large portion of the Hebrew Bible, including the preclassical prophets (e.g., Elijah, Elishah, and Samuel), the classical prophets of the eighth century B.C.E. (e.g., Hosea, Amos, and Isaiah) whose prophecies are preserved in the parallelistic style of Israelite poetry, and the exilic and postexilic prophets (e.g., Jeremiah, 2 Isaiah, and Ezekiel), whose writings reflect a transition in Israelite religion from the days of the monarchy to post-monarchic times.

The prophets were mediators of God's message to Israel, thereby linking heaven to earth just as priests, through ritual activity, link those on earth to heaven. Both seek to maintain and repair the relationship between God and the Israelites, and in several cases (e.g., Samuel, Elijah, Ezekiel) priestly and prophetic roles overlap. The writings of the classical prophets of the eighth century B.C.E. reveal the way in which God's word was perceived to reinforce and demand behavior required by the various law codes, all framed by the notion of covenant.

Related to the covenant is the so-called lawsuit form, a literary genre that is rich in juridical language expressing the following motifs: (a) the calling of witnesses; (b) the accusation of wrongdoing; (c) the sentencing or punishment. In this form, God, acting through the prophet, indicates that Israel has broken the treaty or covenant between them. The language of the court, ancient Israelite legalese of an elegant variety, thus expresses both the relationship between God and Israel and describes breaches of it.

For example, take the opening verses of Isaiah 1, housed in the oracles of the eighth-century B.C.E. Judean prophet. The opening words of the oracle ("Hear O heavens / Pay heed O earth") are a call to witnesses, the heavens and the earth, who were actual deities in threads of ancient Near Eastern thought. Deities are listed as witnesses in the ancient treaty form discussed in connection with covenant. Now they testify to the breaking of Israel's covenant with God. (See also Deut. 32:1 for an illustration of this formulaic chain used to introduce a lawsuit form.) In the worldview of the Israelite prophet Isaiah, "heaven" and "earth" are no longer gods in quite the same sense as in some of the cultures of the ancient Near East, but the nuances of the ancient Near Eastern pattern are intact, such literary clusters being quite conservative and lasting, even allowing for certain theological shifts.

Israel's act of wrongdoing is infidelity to God's covenant in the form of rebellion (2). The punishment is destruction (28). As the chapter now stands, the frame of the lawsuit houses other familiar and traditional literary forms, a "woe oracle" and "cult polemic" that list in greater detail the prophet's view of Israel's wrongdoing. In the former the prophet intones the word "Woe" against "a sinful nation" and describes the sin as "forsaking the Lord." The cult polemic in verses 12–15 rejects Israel's ritual activities as hypocritical, for "your hands are full of blood" (15). The cult polemic does not reject ritual action in general; rather, it suggests that mediation is impossible and forgiveness will be withheld if Israel approaches God without genuine indications of repentance. That upholding the covenant means not only the way one relates to God but the way in which one relates to one's fellow human beings is clear from the following call to repentance:

> Wash, make yourselves clean
> Remove the evil of your deeds
> From before my eyes
> Desist from doing evil
> Learn to do good
> Seek justice
> Transform the ruthless [or "Relieve the oppressed" or "Make the
>   embittered happy"]
> Defend the orphan
> Plead for the widow   (16–17)

Notice the parallelistic style of the prophetic medium, where a line picks up on and adds nuances to the imagery of previous lines, producing an "impressionistic" message (Cross 1974:7) that drives a point home by emphasizing it from many angles. In the Hebrew, the metric scheme also helps to produce the message: the limping meter of the lament (10–15, 21, 28–31), whereby one line of a couplet is longer than its mate, and brief, bold, insistent lines in the call for repentance and transformation, in the manner of a drumbeat (16–17).

The emphasis on ethical treatment of others and the belief that the oppressor can be rehabilitated and transformed is essential to the worldview of the classical prophets and a recurrent theme in other examples of the lawsuit form. Amos, a northern prophet of the eighth century B.C.E., sounds these themes in a lawsuit in 2:6–8. Some sort of ritual and commercial wrongdoing is also condemned (8). The overriding message is clear: while God has upheld his end of the covenant—by destroying Israel's enemies, rescuing her from Egyptian

oppression, and keeping channels of communication open (9–11)—
Israel has repaid God poorly, corrupting the intermediaries (12) and
oppressing the poor (6–7).

The demands of the covenant, faithfulness to God and prescriptions for ethical behavior among people, thus permeate the message
of the eighth-century B.C.E. Israelite prophets, who express the req-
uisites of Yahweh faithfulness, as they understand them, in traditional media. Settings for these oracles may well have been in public
places, performance arenas in which messages were delivered orally.
Perhaps they were outlined in the prophet's mind earlier but were
delivered orally, or perhaps the oracles were composed extempora-
neously through a reliance upon the recurring patterns of language
and content provided by the tradition. A prophet such as Isaiah cri-
tiques hypocritical celebrations of Sabbath or new moons at one of
these very occasions (Isa. 1:13). One can imagine the shock his
speech act would produce. People would gather to rejoice and make
new beginnings, and the prophet would tell them they were mired
in evil. One comprehends how controversial his or her messages
would have been and why the prophets were the self-torturing sub-
versives of the biblical tradition, frequently at odds with the establishment, with those who have the power to oppress. This is true
not only of peripheral prophets such as Amos, who was tied to the
northern monarchy or aristocracy only by the bonds of animus, but
also of Isaiah, who was a central prophet closely associated with the
Davidic monarchs. He is pictured as having particularly close ties to
the southern reforming monarch Hezekiah. The messages of these
prophets, both northern and southern, reveal some of the theological and political tensions of their times, tensions that are described
from the prophet/poets' own perspectives.

The soundings we have taken in Israelite legal and ethical texts, themselves soundings from a larger and multiform tradition of custom and
law, reveal both some of the synchronic, shared aspects of Israelite
tradition and interesting implicit tensions and developments.

All of the materials explored express a staunch Yahweh alonism.
This is not to suggest that even the ancient Israelites who prepared

these texts did not believe in the existence of other deities, but that their God was the most powerful, the only one they were to worship. Throughout we have seen the importance of covenant as a means of defining the group in its relationship with God. Fealty to the divine covenant partner involves not only loyalty to Yahweh alone, but adherence to ethical demands governing human behavior and to a set of ritual and priestly prescriptions and proscriptions.

Care for the poor and the less fortunate is a feature of each corpus, even including the priestly, aristocratically generated materials of Leviticus. The poor are to be allowed to glean, and corners of the field are to be left unharvested for their benefit (Leviticus 19:9–10, 23:22). None of the collections assumes that poverty will be eradicated; all assume that the battle with injustice is ongoing.

From polemics against certain practices, we learn what some Israelite considered to be features of their Yahwism: worship of deities other than Yahweh; practices surrounding the dead that imply their continuing capacity to inform, benefit, or harm the living; various divinatory practices; fertility rituals; and child sacrifice.

Do the codes reflect and reveal the actions and expectations of actual Israelites? As noted in chapter 1, archaeological information sometimes tallies with a biblical author's projections or assumptions. The agricultural worker of Metsad Hashavyyahu who wishes to send a letter of complaint to the authorities appears to know his rights, that it is contrary to custom or law to withhold a person's garment taken in pledge overnight (Exod. 22:26–27 [Hebrew 25–26]; Deut. 24:12–13, 17). Inscriptional material associating Ashera, a female deity, with Yahweh in a positive or neutral way may explain the polemics of Deut. 16:21 and Mic. 5:12–13 [Hebrew 13–14].

The codes seem to track a chronology through pre-monarchic, monarchic, and post-monarchic periods, though each code overlaps all or some of these major segments of Israelite history. The Ten Commandments, for example, contain universal and timeless expectations for ethical human behavior that strengthen and uphold society, as well as specifically Israelite expectations about Yahweh faithfulness. The anionic theme of Exodus 20 points to a particular Judean thread that dominates the cult of the central Jerusalem temple, while the emphasis on the Sabbath becomes especially strong in the post-monarchic or second-temple period as a means of self-definition and self-identification in the absence of an independent land, kingship, and other aspects of the preexilic Israelite symbol system. Thus, within the Ten Commandments one sees hints of a span of Israelite worldviews as well as synchronic aspects of the tradition and universal interests shared with human societies from a wide array of cultures.

In its essentials the Covenant Code in Exodus may well stem from the highland culture that precedes the monarchy, whereas Deuteronomic materials react to and try to circumscribe the power of kings. The Deuteronomic corpus exudes a strongly us–them attitude that betokens a perception that society is stressed and under siege. This attitude may be as old as northern Levitical circles disenfranchised with the Jeroboam schism and as late as the troubles of the exile. Priestly material in Leviticus quintessentially expresses the concern with order and chaos at work in the other codes as well. Defining the world in terms of clean and unclean becomes a formative thread in Rabbinic Judaism and is rooted in priestly concerns of those who must mediate between the realms of divine and human. Such concerns, which may be as ancient as pre-monarchic priestly groups working at decentralized shrines, reflect the worldview of the Jerusalem-based central priesthood of the monarchy and their postexilic successors.

SUGGESTED READINGS

On covenant, see the works by Mendenhall and Hillers.

For an introduction to law in a biblical context, see the essay by Greenstein in *Back to the Sources* (1984), ed. Holtz. See also Carmichael's, *Origins of Biblical Law* (1992).

For additional examples of ancient Near Eastern treaties, see Pritchard's *Ancient Near Eastern Texts* (1969).

On the worldview of the Deuteronomic writers see the article by Stulman and Carmichael's *Laws of Deuteronomy* (1974).

On biblical law and women, see the essays by Bird, Pressler's *View of Women*

Found in the Deuteronomic Family Laws (1993), and Carmichael's *Women, Law, and the Genesis Traditions* (1979).

In recent years a number of scholars have begun to explore, with interesting results, biblical law from the perspective of the law professor. See the works by Miller. Also of interest is the work of Hibbitts, who explores nonverbal aspects of legal traditions in traditional cultures.

5

The Ritual Dimension

If the legal dimension of Israelite religion seeks to impose a patina of order on the problematical and chaos-prone nature of human existence, the ritual dimension serves to restore the image of order when it falls into disarray or becomes clouded. Ritual also may symbolize certain aspects of God's creation, dynamically and metonymically helping to recreate the cosmos on a regular, periodic basis or at critical junctures in the lives of individuals or the life of the community. Ritual is about status, the shaping and reshaping of status.

In the following examples we explore: (1) the ritual that yearly recreates Israel's founding in the events of the exodus, a ritual held within each family and household in a decentralized and democratized fashion (Exodus 12); (2) a ritual of atonement whereby the high priest attempts to rid the community of sin (Leviticus 16); (3) a ritual process to deal with a socially disruptive source of uncertainty, a case in which a woman is accused by her husband of adultery without recourse to eyewitnesses (Numbers 5:11–31); and (4) a ritual of maturation involving adolescent women (Judg. 11:29–40).

As in exploring versions of Israelite myths or legal collections, one hopes to be able to set the material within specific time frames and settings in the lengthy Israelite tradition. The procedures for specific named offerings outlined in some detail in Leviticus, for example, the well-being offering, the reparations (or guilt) offering, the purification (or sin) offering, were essential and routine features of ritual life at the Jerusalem temple. The mediators of such rituals were members of a hereditary priesthood trained in the requisite skills of slaughter, flaying, cutting, and so on. That animal sacrifice in some form was a central feature of pre-monarchic Israel is also certain, though scenes portraying altar-building and animal-sacrificing pre-monarchic heroes, rich in local color, are more difficult to situate specifically. The home-based Passover in Exodus 12 surely predates attempts to centralize sacrificial worship in Jerusalem during the Southern monarchies, though such celebrations of Passover no doubt continued in spite of the political preferences of kings such as Hezekiah and Josiah and the theological preferences of their Deuteronomistic supporters.

Synchronic Matters

Certain attitudes and symbols seem to maintain their meaning throughout the tradition. Perhaps one of the most pervasive themes— and the one which is most shocking to a modern Western reader—is the value placed upon blood and blood sacrifice. Although some ceremonial actions in ancient Israel involve the offering of grain and some involve other ritual activities such as marching in procession, playing musical instruments, singing, letting the hair grow over a lengthy period of time, or undertaking a period of isolation, many, perhaps most rituals involve the killing of animals and the splashing, spattering, and daubing of blood. Read, for example, Lev. 8:18–24 that describes the use of blood in the ordination ceremony for priests. One can imagine the amount of blood let and flesh roasted during the heyday of the Jerusalem temple in the upkeep of the various regular and occasional offerings outlined in Leviticus. Think of the various aromas, some good, some requiring covering up by incense. Think of the agricultural economy required to supply the temple and God's perceived need for blood sacrifice.

Blood is a vital substance in Israelite religious life, holding a critical place in narrative and performative aspects of the tradition. Blood is capable of purifying, mediating, and contaminating, depending upon the context and circumstances. It is, to use anthropologist Victor Turner's phrase, a "multivocalic symbol," that is, a symbol having the capacity for multiple, even contradictory, meanings. The blood of menstruation (as was noted in chap. 3) is unclean rendering, while the blood of the bull of the sin-offering purifies when applied to the horns of the sacrificial altar.

Blood must not be eaten but must be poured on the ground at the ritual slaughter of animals, for the life force is in the blood and the ruddy earth itself must absorb it into herself. Indeed the sound-alike terms for "earth," *'ădāmāh*, "red," *'ādōm*, "blood," *dām*, and "human," *'ādām* provide the biblical writers ample opportunity for wordplay that encapsulates complex symbolic patterns in Israelite belief. The redness of blood as symbolic of the human, earthbound side of the mortal–divine dichotomy comes to extend to other ritual items involved in the relationship between humans and God. A good example is the pure red heifer whose ashes are a critical ingredient in the water of purification. This medium allows those who have had physical contact with the dead to be cleansed, that is, to make the transition from the realm of the dead, with whom they have had visceral contact, to the realm of the living (Numbers 19) and to a condition of wholeness that allows them to approach God. The one who has touched death is rehabilitated by cleansing water mixed with this intensified, burnt down, life-containing medium of red ashes.

Blood symbolizes not only the presence of the earthy life force but also the sacrifice of something of value on the part of humans who would propitiate or seek the deity. The blood suggests a deity who appreciates such sacrifice, the savory aroma of roasted flesh, a deity satiated by the blood at his altar. Perhaps this is to overliteralize and yet surely such ideas lurk not far beneath the surface of Israelite thought. It is, I would argue, such a notion of God's desires that leads

to one Israelite ideology of war in which the enemy dead are vowed
to God in return for victory, thereby justifying massive killing. (Niditch 1993a:28–55) It is, after all, blood smeared on the doorposts of
Israelite homes that turns away (or satisfies) God in his role as destroyer in Exodus.

Exodus 12

For those readers who were raised as Jews and are used to the rhythms
and contents of the Jewish liturgical calendar, Exodus 12 contains
much that is familiar. It is the biblical founding text for the festival of
Passover, celebrating Israel's escape from Egyptian oppression and
slavery. God's command to Moses relayed to the Israelites to prepare
a special Passover meal, to eat bitter herbs and unleavened bread, to
keep the custom of eating unleavened bread for a week, the first and
last days being special holy days when one is to refrain from work,
the emphasis on family and the group, the remembrance of God's
rescue, and the need to teach one's children about these saving events
(24–27) are all rooted in the traditions preserved in Exodus 12. Within
the biblical narrative, Exodus 12 is the first Passover to be revisited
and recreated each spring. And yet there is much that may be less
modern, familiar, or comfortable. When we examine the ritual and its
pattern of symbols more closely, we discover ways in which this ritual
partakes of ancient Israelite worldview.

First, of course, is the emphasis on animal sacrifice: a lamb without
blemish, a year-old male from the sheep or the goats. The lamb is to
be no bigger than that which a household can completely consume.
If a household is too small to consume a whole lamb, it is to join with
its neighbor to slaughter and consume the lamb, a portion reserved
for each member of the group. The household (*bêt 'āb*) refers to an
extended family as described in the introduction; the emphasis on
kinship is strong. All of these kin groups are to slaughter their animal
at twilight, the passage time when one status ends and another begins.
(recall the discussion of clean versus unclean in chap. 4) The blood
of the lamb is to be daubed on the lintel and doorposts of each house
in which it is eaten, a signal to Yahweh to pass over Israelite homes

when he "executes judgment on all the gods of Egypt," striking down the firstborn in Egypt (12:12). The lamb itself is to be roasted whole, with its head, legs, and inner organs intact. It is to be eaten that very night together with bitter herbs and unleavened bread. Anything that remains until morning shall be burned. Israelites are to eat this meal hurriedly, girded, wearing sandals, and with staff in hand (11). No uncircumcised person may join in the meal, thus excluding aliens who are not Yahwists, members of the covenant.

Some of these symbols in the ritual pattern are explained within the passage itself: the bread is unleavened because the Israelites had to leave quickly (39); likewise the prescriptions for dress and behavior during the meal (11). The blood is a sign of God's passing or skipping over Israelite homes (according to the folk etymology at v. 13), during the night, when God as Destroyer is abroad.

In the tradition's own glosses and in the orders to Moses, one begins to notice quite a difference between the sentiments and emotions aroused in ancient celebrants of the Passover and the feelings and ambience we experience as modern participants. We enjoy a leisurely, delicious meal in which we recline like kings, taking the time to reflect upon shared history and values. They are frightened, their hearts race; they have to eat in haste. Perhaps only Jews who celebrated Passover with the threat of Nazis or pogroms outside their door could experience those earlier emotions. And what of the meal?

As was noted, sacrifice is the central feature of Israelite ritual life, a means of mediating the relationship between God and humans by offering up something of value, as well as a means of mediating between people who share in a portion of this precious food source.

The slaughtering of animals is not undertaken lightly. Ancient Israelites do not purchase meat, precut and prepackaged in plastic, so that they forget that it once was part of a warm, living being. Rather, the shedding of blood is made sacred, undertaken in a prescribed fashion. Meat eating takes place in a sacred setting (see, e.g., 1 Sam. 9:12–13, 14:33–35) that leads to an awareness of what one has done. The meal bonds in special ritual ties those who share the being who was once alive in order that they might enjoy themselves and be strong. While Deuteronomic attempts to centralize sacrifice seem to allow for a partial desacralization of meat eating (Deut. 12:15, 21–22), rules concerning the special treatment of the animal's blood remain strong even in Deuteronomic tradition (Deut. 12:16, 23).

What is easily overlooked if one does not try to identify with the ancient Israelites is how unusual the sacrificial meal of the Passover is within the ancient Israelite context. I have mentioned the haste—no songs or timbrels here, no enjoyment. In contrast to usual meat-eating practices in a sacrificial context, the slaughtered animal is not flayed, quartered, or arranged in pieces upon the altar, its entrails and legs washed (Lev. 1:6–9); nor is the meat boiled as in normal practice (Lev. 6:28 [Hebrew 6:21]; Ezek. 46: 20,24; Num. 6:19; Exod. 29:31; Zech. 14:21; 1 Sam. 2:13). Rather, the slaughtered animal is roasted whole, with its entrails intact. All of it is, moreover, roasted or burned by fire, a method of preparation generally used for God's portion of an offering or for the "burnt offering" which is totally consumed by fire except for the hide, which is given to the priest (Lev. 1; 7:8). The mode of preparation is thus basic, simple, close to nature. No pots of boiling water intervene, only a stick and fire being necessary. No culturally sanctioned prepreparation of the animal is allowed. The eating of unleavened bread further contributes to this image of eating simply and close to nature, for the bread does not undergo the process of fermentation and refinement that leavening implies. Finally, the bitter herbs are less a variety of food than vegetation, and while some scholars have suggested that these herbs were a condiment of sorts, uses of the Hebrew root *mar* (bitter) in the Bible seem to point to something unpleasant rather than piquant: "gall," "poison," "a bitter thing" (e.g., Lam. 3:15).

This meal, then, is a sober, unbanquetlike repast marking a rite of passage or transition from the status of slaves to the status of free men and women. The midpoint of this passage, as in so many rites of passage in other cultures, is marked by a stripping down to basics, a sensation of moving quickly, accompanied by emotions of trepidation appropriate to those taking a required and perilous journey. And yet the Israelite ritual passengers are not alone. They eat roasted flesh in a communion with the deity, who himself usually claims the burned portions. They bond with one another, eating all of a whole lamb (or burning the rest) at the same time. No noncircumcised aliens are allowed, and the participants are enclosed in households, all bounded by the sign of blood. As in other rituals, the blood, this multivocal symbol, sanctifies and purifies the house, a boundary marker between Egyptians and Israelites, between those who will suffer a death in their families, the disruption of the male line of descent, and those who will be given life. Blood is the life force, but it also connotes the loss of life and sacrifice.

Where does one place Exodus 12 in the complicated trajectories of Israelite history and worldview explored in chapter 1? The special meaning of blood, bread, and roasted flesh emerges from the pan-Israelite tradition preserved in the Hebrew Bible, and usages in Exodus 12 are not easily datable to one time. It seems possible that Exodus 12 is a very early ritual that served to bond the Israelites, to define them as a whole, sharing and reenacting a foundation myth that perhaps reflects a historical memory of some elements of the group that would become Israel. The household-and kinship-based nature of the enactment testifies to the importance of that unit throughout Israel's history. Such family groupings could serve as ritual centers without the need for elaborate altars, temples, hereditary personnel, and the various accoutrements of an urban center such as Jerusalem or even of a smaller frontier outpost such as Arad. Some scholars suggest that festivals of Passover and unleavened bread were once separate. By the time the traditions in Exodus 12 have coalesced, they are one, and it is difficult to glimpse the world that may have preceded this coalescence.

Various Southern pro-centralization voices in the Bible, those behind Deuteronomy and 1 and 2 Chronicles, preferred that the ancient festival become a state ritual, performed in the great temple in Jerusalem and controlled by priests (see Deut. 16:2, 5–6; 2 Chronicles 30 [Hezekiah's Passover]; 2 Chronicles 35 [Josiah's Passover]). It is possible that actual Judean kings felt likewise, for such rituals would enhance their power and prestige. Even the Chronicler suggests, however, that many, especially in the North, laughed at requests to centralize Passover (2 Chron. 30:10–11), perhaps reflecting a more realistic assessment of how successful such attempts were. It is too simplistic to suggest that the view of Passover in Exodus 12 reflects pre-monarchic times and the view in Deuteronomy 16 the monarchy, perhaps the reform under Josiah. Rather, the democratizing Passover of Exodus 12 reflects the continuing vitality of kinship communities throughout Israel's history. The holiday is celebrated in one's own community and household, where all share equally in the food; no special portions belong to the priest (contrast, e.g., Lev. 7:31–34, 6:26 [Hebrew 6:22], 7:1–6), and no priest is necessary to do the slaughtering

Leviticus 16

In contrast to Exodus 12, Leviticus 16 describes a ritual in which the high priest is central to the successful completion of ritual action and thereby central to the health of the community whose well-being depends upon proper mediation between humans and God.

In the biblical context of the wilderness wanderings, Leviticus 16 contains directions from God to be delivered by Moses to his brother Aaron. God first directs Moses to tell Aaron that he must not enter the inner sanctuary behind the curtain at any time he chooses. Appearances in God's holy place must be safely fenced off and bounded. When Aaron does come, he must prepare himself properly.

Leviticus 16 describes a critical annual ceremony that cleanses the people of all their sins. This set of actions allows the community so cleansed a fresh start in its relationship with God and with one another. The priestly code, of course, provides for a host of other regular purification and reparation offerings brought by people and mediated through priests, but this particular ceremony, like the Passover, is pictured as a pan-Israelite event that gives everyone a fresh start, presumably covering any wrongdoing or sources of uncleanness that may have been missed in other ritual actions. It takes place on the tenth day of the New Year's month of Tishre and is an ancient precursor of Yom Kippur. In this celebration the high priest's role is unique and central.

Sacrifice and the purificatory capacities of blood and water again play key roles, and the hereditary Aaronid priest is adept at the manipulation of these substances. He must obey boundaries and rules, entering the inner sanctuary, the holy place, only as directed; he is to dress in special linen garments after purifying himself by bathing. Preliminaries involve the selection of sacrificial animals. Aaron is to begin his sacrificial ministrations by offering a bull as a purification offering for himself and his household. The one who seeks atonement for the community must himself be pure. He also prepares two goats. Aaron presents them to Yahweh before the tent of meeting, the locus for divine–human mediation, the place where God allows his spirit to enter.

Lots are cast to determine the fate of the goats. As elsewhere in the Hebrew Bible and the wider ancient Near East, the casting of lots is a mode of determining the will of God, the gods, or fate. It is means of allowing forces beyond human reason to determine the actions one should take in a situation of uncertainty. For example, lots are cast to determine who is guilty of breaking God's covenant in the Achan incident (Josh. 7:14–18) and in the honey-eating incident (1 Sam. 14: 41–42). In this case it is to be determined which goat is designated for which function in the ritual, for one goat will be sacrificed to Yahweh (Lev. 16:8) and the other will be sent live into the wilderness to "Azazel." This term, generally translated "scapegoat," may derive from *'az 'el* (god is strong). It has been suggested that Azazel was a wilderness deity, a threatening power that had to be appeased in an ancient pre-Israelite ritual. Others derive the etymology from *'āzal*, meaning "to go away," the notion being that the animal leaves or is entirely removed.

The bull that atones for Aaron and his household is offered first. This process of purification involves slaughtering the animal and then making a smokescreen with fired coals and incense in the most sacred portion of the tent behind the curtain that divides holy from holier (12). The smoke is, in fact, meant to blanket the covering, or "mercy seat," that is upon the ark of the testimony (13), a sort of ground zero for God's divine presence, the traditional container for the commandments of the covenant dictated to Moses or, in some threads of the tradition, written by the finger of God himself. Notice the distancing here, as in the Israelites' stance at Mount Sinai (Exodus 19). There the people are not to approach beyond a certain point lest God's explosive power burst forth against them. Here even the high priest approaches with caution. Smoke masks the covering that signifies the holy locus. Only then does Aaron dare to approach. If the layer fails, he dies. In this priestly ritual dimension, the power of Yahweh shimmers and terrifies, an electric force field capable of extinguishing mortals, even those who belong to a hereditary priesthood and who are in a state of ritual purity. The priest sprinkles some of the blood of the bull on the front of the covering seven times, blood in its capacity to purify and mediate, seven being a prime, holy number signifying wholeness in the priestly tradition.

Then comes the slaughtering of the goat designated by lot for slaughter. Its blood is brought into the holy sanctuary behind the curtain and is sprinkled in the same fashion as the blood of the bull. With this action, the priest purifies the tent of meeting, the outer room, and the sanctuary, the "adytum" or inner room (16). The purifying blood of the bull and the goat is then to be applied to the horns of the altar. Again the blood is sprinkled with the finger seven times. That which is cleansed is not only the possible contamination conveyed by droplets of "the unclean" (*ṭāmē'*) in the place of supreme holiness but also sin itself, transgression of God's covenant (16, 19) (*pešaʿ, ḥēt'*), which is a form of uncleanness. As discussed in chapter 4, transgression can take the form of inhumanity, cultic infraction, or any neglect of the covenant with God. Sin, like the seductive personification in the story of Cain and Abel, the one who crouches at the door, is real and visceral, a contaminant which makes impossible a healthful continuation of the covenant community, a poison that must be purged from the body of the community.

Now that the sacred loci have been cleaned, the ritual that cleanses the people can proceed. Aaron lays his hands upon the goat designated for Azazel and confesses upon it (lit. "causes to be cast out," "thrown out in public") all the transgressions of the people. Notice the piling up in verse 21 of terms for sin. In a sympathetic magical process, the sins are invested in the goat, which is led into the wilderness. The sins of the people literally course through the priest's hands and voice and onto the goat. The goat then takes sin with him beyond the group's borders and body politic. At the close of the ceremonies of atonement involving two goats comes an inclusio, an echo and mirror image of the opening actions. Aaron enters the tent of meeting, removes his holy linen garments, bathes himself in water in a holy place, and puts his daily clothes back on. Then he again offers a burnt offering to atone for himself and the people. As he made a passage into holiness with bathing, dressing, and sacrificing, so he makes a passage out of the most sacred realm. Even though the priest, on some level, is always of the sacred realm, sacredness also has its degrees of holiness and its hierarchies in this priestly worldview.

The blood of the bull and the goat cleanses and atones. The animals that have given their blood for atonement must now be consumed in fire: their fat turned into smoke on the altar (25), their skin, flesh, and dung immolated outside the camp. The one who has set free the goat for "Azazel" bathes outside the camp and then may enter, for he has touched the goat which, through sympathetic magic, has come to contain sin. The one who burns the goat and bull must also wash his clothes, bathe his body in water and then enter. A passage of cleansing is also necessary for him in order that he return to the mundane world. The animals, their blood drawn, have become somehow dangerous, capable of contaminating. They cannot be eaten or employed in some practical fashion; only the fat is offered to God. In this case sacrifice involves significant financial loss.

Lev. 16:29–34 further frames the ritual: its date is the tenth of Tishre, the current day for Yom Kippur in the Jewish calendar; there is the command not to work for Israelites and resident aliens (as in the first and last days of Passover); and there is the command to "afflict" oneself, which in the classical and modern tradition has been interpreted to mean fasting. A summary is found at verses 32–33, reviewing some of the essentials of the atonement ritual. Scholars have suggested that verses 29–34 reflect a later framework. These verses situate an atonement ceremony—perhaps enacted during times of particular crisis and performed only by the high priest—as a yearly festival in which all can participate through fasting and cessation of work.

Even in its current form, the ritual emphasizes the absolutely central role of the priest. Only through him and the ministrations in which he is trained can the community be purified and absolved. This ritual further illustrates the power of blood as a multivocalic symbol, the capacity of blood and water to alter an unclean status, and the role of sympathetic magic in Israelite ritual as sins are transferred from people to priest to goat to oblivion. It also emphasizes the visceral power of uncleanness and sin. Finally, this ritual beautifully illustrates a particular hierarchical worldview; levels of holiness characterize the architecture of sacred spaces, and only the purified priest dare enter after careful preparations. This is a hierarchical worldview in which God is supremely transcendent and in which the status of priest as mediator elevates him above the rest of the community. The central role of Levitical priests in a certain thread of Israelite culture and other important issues in Israelite worldview emerge in the ritual description at Num. 5:11–31.

Numbers 5:11–31

This ritual, like others in Leviticus and Numbers, is presented as a word of God to Moses. In contrast to Exodus 12 and Leviticus 16, the situation requiring the ritual involves possible individual transgression within a family context. A wife is accused of committing adultery and no witnesses are available to testify to her guilt or innocence. And yet the matter is settled publicly and becomes a community-wide issue. In this worldview, clearly demarcated patrilineages are critical to the social order (see Eilberg-Schwartz 1990). It is more difficult to prove who is the father than who is the mother of a child. In a strongly patrilineal structure in which lines of descent reflect not only one's personal identity but also one's economic and political status, it is critical that all agree upon which child belongs to which father. As Eilberg-Schwartz (1990) has shown, the Israelites are obsessed with male lines of descent and their writings reflect a visceral need to keep lines pure or to prove that they are pure. Adultery threatens to mix up the seeds, to destabalize the system.

The family is a microcosm for society as a whole, and problems within one family threaten the social fabric. The accusation that is not resolved may indeed lead to violence and vengeance, as the woman's own family rallies to her support and the man's family to his. The matter is thus placed in God's hands through the ministrations of his priest.

This passage is written by men for men, by those who depict a strongly androcentric society, one in which the woman is presumed guilty unless proven innocent through divine intervention. In this culture the priestly mediator is male, the husband accuses and suffers no penalty for false accusation, and the accused wife is symbolically stripped and humiliated. She is quintessentially a womb that must be kept available and pure to grow her husband's seed.

Notice first in the frame for the ritual, the assumption in verses 11–14a that the accused woman is guilty but not provably so. Only in verse 14b—and almost as an afterthought in the rhetorical flow of the passage—is it suggested that the "spirit of jealousy" may come upon the man even if she has not defiled herself. The term for defile or be unclean (*ṭāmē'*) is the same term employed for food that is not kosher and for the condition that must be wiped away in the ritual of atonement in Leviticus 16 (see v. 16 on the tent of meeting and sanctuary contaminated by people's uncleanness). The concept is one of clean verses unclean, remaining within proper categories or boundaries verses being outside the boundary, marginal, or disruptive.

The husband brings his accused wife to the priest. He has brought a small grain offering. In contrast to other grain offerings, the grain is not enhanced with oil and frankincense but kept in its most simple natural form. Moreover, the offering consists of barley, flour of a lower-quality than the choice flour called *qemaḥ* (Lev. 2:1, 6:14–15; [Hebrew 6:13–14]). It is described as an offering of jealousy, of remembrance that causes sin to be remembered. This basic grain, as designated, contains the potential to unmask the iniquity, to expose it. The grain is also a symbol of fertility or sexuality. The seedy, coarse yet fecund nature of barley, in fact, is invoked beautifully in the book of Ruth to represent that nubile woman's ripe sexuality (see Feeley-Harnik 1990:171).

The accused woman is "set before Yahweh," brought to the central shrine. The priest creates a liquid concoction of holy water and dust from the floor of the tabernacle, the place where God allows his spirit to dwell. Again the essential substances of water and earth combine.

The woman herself is made by the priest to hold the grain offering in her hands; he later offers a portion upon the altar and dishevels her hair (lit. "lets go," "lets loose," or "unbinds" her hair). A person's hair—its length, its style, whether it is worn covered or not, bound or loose—is a significant marker in any traditional culture. For example, young woman often wear their hair one way, mature women another. It has been suggested that the dishevelment of the woman's hair is a sign of mourning (as in Lev. 10:6, 21:10) or of the leper, the one who, like a mourner, wears torn clothing, dishevels his hair, and cries "Unclean, unclean" (Lev. 13:45). All three instances of loosing the hair imply a removal from society, from normal social status, a self-debasement. In this case, having a male priest unbind the woman's hair is more than an altering of her status, a removal from society, or a declaration of uncleanness. It is also an exposure. Like the grain, the woman is brought forward in a natural state, unadorned and uncovered. The truth, like the grain and the woman herself, is to be uncovered. That the loosing of her hair is a sort of unveiling cannot be doubted, and for a feminist reader it reflects the woman's powerlessness in a world of men.

The woman is made to take an oath: if no man has lain with her besides her husband, she will be immune to the "water of bitterness" that she will drink; if she is guilty, the water will literally cause her thigh (womb) to drop and her belly (uterus) to swell. She becomes, moreover, an outcast, an execration among her people. Indeed, the rejected woman, the widow, and the barren woman are all marginal. The woman accused of adultery suffers an additional sort of marginality in a world that permits only two sorts of women: the virgin in her father's home and the child-bearing faithful wife who lives under the protection of her husband. The words of the priest evidence a rhythmic parallelism in content and syntax, as befits an adjuration. A most interesting portion of the ceremony is described at 5:23–24. The priest writes the words of the curse on a document and then literally wipes them or washes them into the water of bitterness. Then the woman is made to drink the water of the curse. Thus the words carry the power of their meaning into the potion that dissolves and absorbs them. In this world curses and blessings are real, having the capacity to bring about their content, and written words and letters have a special transformative magic power. The woman literally takes the curse within her, but it has power over her only if she is guilty. Such a view of writing belongs to those who do not take writing for granted. The same view of writing emerges in the scene of the writing on the wall in Daniel 5 and in the initiation of the prophet Ezekiel, who swallows the scroll containing God's words, thereby becoming his prophet, a man who is filled with the messages of the deity in a quite physical or visceral fashion (3:1–3). The skills of writing are thus framed by an oral mentality.

The priest burns a portion of the grain offering on the altar, sending it heavenward in the form of smoke; the deity is thereby invoked. The earthy substance becomes an airy substance. A symbol of the woman's sexuality is offered to the male deity, who is the ultimate judge, deciding whether this fertility has been properly used. The trial by water proceeds; if the woman is guilty, she suffers the curses as described. Note that the suffering affects the reproductive organs in just-desserts fashion. If she suffers no ill effect, she is to be rehabilitated as clean and will have children. This ceremony, like the law of the Levirite (Deut. 25:5–10) or laws concerning raped women, is meant to keep androcentric categories in order, to deal with cases of females who no longer fit the proper categories for mature women. The woman's feelings have nothing to do with the matter. Women are a valuable commodity to be properly stored and utilized. Mishandled goods have to be eliminated or somehow repackaged in order that the system be maintained. Within the contours of this system, such laws may, however, be a woman's only protection, especially in the hands of a sympathetic priest.

If a woman is innocent, she may be cleared of accusation and the husband must take her back and set aside his jealousy; pressure from his peers and the belief system force him to do so. Would a woman desire to be married to an obsessively jealous husband or to her rapist, as the law allows? One doubts it, but without the marriage she becomes a castaway, permanently outside social boundaries in a small world in which social boundaries are virtually requisite for survival.

This ritual reveals how a society in which priestly practitioners are regarded as central deals with one source of rupture. Symbols of water, dust, grain, and hair—all of which are presented in a basic, natural state—combine with the visceral power of words, as understood by the illiterate, to effect the resolution of a crisis. The crisis is precipitated because of the culture's particular views of social structure and the place of women within it. Such issues in gender are, in fact, central to the social dimension of Israelite worldview.

A Ritual from the Woman's Point of View: Judges 11:29–40

Whereas Num. 5:11–31 describes a crisis involving a woman in this androcentric and patrilineal society from the man's point of view, Judg. 11:29–40 reveals an ancient Israelite ritual for women and provides a foundation myth that can be understood more from the young woman's point of view. This is not to suggest that the tale of Jephthah's daughter is any less androcentric than Numbers 5, only that within the contours of this system the ritual acknowledges the young woman's anxieties during a critical time in her life. The ritual helps to comfort her by emphasizing the community of young women of similar age and is grounded in a foundation story that underscores her pathos in a world ruled by men.

The narrative plot of Judg. 11:29–40 that serves as a founding myth for the ritual is rooted in ancient Israelite war ideologies. If the warrior vows something valuable to the deity—even the sacrifice of a human or humans, the most valuable resource—then it is expected that in return the deity will assist the hero in achieving victory. This belief lies behind the Israelite ban in which the enemy is vowed to Yahweh in total destruction (see Num. 21:1–3; cf. Niditch 1993a, chap. 2) and underlies Jephthah's vow before a battle with the Ammonites. "If you truly give the Ammonites into my hand, then whatever emerges from the doors of my house to meet me in my victorious return from the Ammonites shall be for Yahweh and I will offer it up as a burnt offering" (Judg. 11:30–31). Jephthah is victorious; what emerges from his house is no he-goat or young bull but his daughter, his only child, who greets him, in the woman's way, with timbrels and dancing. While the phrase "that which emerges" is neutral and could refer to anyone or anything, the audience of this traditional tale surely knew how the story would proceed, much as classical Greek audiences knew that Oedipus would kill his father. A modern listener or reader of "Beauty and the Beast" similarly knows that the merchant's daughter, Beauty, will be sent to Beast to atone for the rose when, according to some versions of the tale, he makes the very demand required by Jephthah's vow: "Give me the first thing you see upon your return" (see Brown 1978).

Shared knowledge of the story of Jephthah helps to create pathos and participation in his sad plight, thereby reinforcing shared values and beliefs. Feminist scholars and other literary critics understandably ask how Jephthah could be so rash in making his vow. Surely he knew that the young girl would be the first to greet his victory, as was customary. Does the story of Jephthah reflect a world in which the war vow was an accepted feature of waging war, in which human sacrifice in this context was a possibility? Is the author presenting what he considers to be the past, a time when strange customs governed human behavior? Did the Israelite past actually contain such a world, or do such stories of child sacrifice and human-desiring deities reflect not reality but deep-seated features of human psychology?

The author of Judges 11 surely believed such a world existed, and it has recently been suggested by many scholars that human sacrifice was indeed a feature of state religion in Israel until the seventh-century B.C.E. reforms of King Josiah (see J. Day; Heider 1985; Niditch 1993b). To their credit, the framers of the Hebrew Bible condemn the practice, but the concept of the efficacy of human sacrifice and the notion of God's appreciation for these valuable offerings continue in the tradition in various forms.

In Judges 11 the sacrifice vowed and offered to God becomes a model for and a symbolic mirror of a woman's life passages. The tale does not send the message that women should be offered as burnt sacrifices to God; rather, it suggests that every young woman about to make the transition from her father to her husband, from virginity to a life of conjugal relations, from childhood to motherhood is on some level to confront Beauty's Beast. She is to be sacrificed, leaving the safety of home and patrilineal relations to go to someone else's patrilineage. The emphasis in the tale shifts from issues of war and victory and the costs that God exacts for victory to concern over the young woman's passage from childhood to adulthood. Thus, Jephthah's daughter receives permission from her father to go with her friends and "cry over her virginity" for two months (11:37). They are going to wander (so Greek manuscript traditions) in the mountains for two months and then she will face her fate.

Peggy Day and others (Walls 1992:158–59) have noted that the term translated above as "virginity" and related to the more common biblical term for a maiden, *bĕtûlāh*, need not only refer to a woman's status as virgin but also to her age and time in life. The *bĕtûlāh* is of marriageable age but not yet bearing children in marriage, as would adult women in this traditional culture. P. Day suggests that Judges 11:40 describes a maturation ritual whereby young, unmarried women join to lament Jephthah's daughter. The rite of passage marking the movement from the status of nubile young woman to that of married adult thus includes a liminal, betwixt-and-between stage involving isolation, building of community among the ritual passengers, and ritual mourning. The specifics of this ritual are rooted in an ancient Israelite myth, but the general contours of the ritual pattern and the existence of such maturation rituals are common in many cultures (see P. Day 1989).

The equation of human sacrifice with marriage may seem a shocking one. Indeed, for the modern reader a neutral or uncritical acknowledgment that Israelites believed that Yahweh could desire and accept humans in sacrifice is stunning. In attempting to identify with ancient Israelites, one might suggest that while the myth is violent and troubling, the ritual implies a certain empathy for young women within the contours of a particular social structure and its symbol system. The system and its worldview are not challenged in the biblical text of Judges 11, and we may find the story offensive. The ritual acknowledges, however, that transitions in a woman's life are fearful and evoke unhappy emotions, that the support of one's childhood friends is important, and that the young woman and her family may well regard her new husband and his family as fearful Others.

This ritual requires no priest and speaks to relationships in kinship and marriage that probably characterized Israelite social structure since the earliest pre-monarchic times. That such a ritual would have remained meaningful to Israelite women long after the early settlement period is entirely possible, given that patterns of kinship and marriage remain important throughout Israelite history.

Four soundings in Israelite law reveal both continuity and variation in Israelite religion. As in all ritual, the ceremonies as described effect transformation, allowing for changes in status: slave and disparate to free and unified; unclean to clean; suspect to convicted or rehabilitated; adolescent to adult. The grounding of these repeated dramatic religious patterns in Israelite sacred stories makes each Passover, Day of Atonement, or trial by water a return to essentials, to beginnings, a reminder of who Israel is and how she stands in a lengthy, continuous tradition with the ancestor-heroes and ancestor-heroines of earlier times.

Certain symbols recur throughout the tradition, for example, the blood and water that cleanse and alter one's status. The dichotomy between the natural and the cultural are symbolized in some form in each of the rituals described: the nonprocessed food of Passover versus leavened bread and boiled meat; the wilderness for the goat that swallows up sin versus the newly purified cultural community; the woman's unbound hair that exposes her without the cosmetic veils of human invention; the period spent in the mountains, a respite in nature's realm, before taking on the cultural responsibilities of wife and mother. Throughout, the deity is one who demands sacrifice, usually blood sacrifice but sometimes human beings, the most valuable sacrifice of all.

And yet these four soundings reveal different threads in Israelite worldview that may relate to differing periods or voices in the cultural tradition. The ritual of atonement (Leviticus 16) and the ritual for women accused of adultery (Num. 5:11–31) stem from priestly sources for whom the role of priest as mediator between God and humans is absolutely essential. Also important is a central shrine where he practices his craft. Exodus 12, the Passover, and the ceremony for nubile young women (Judges 11) require no priest and are community-based rituals that can be performed in any hill town or village. This distinction is not necessarily a chronological one, for Passover and ceremonies for young women who have reached maturity could well coexist with more centralized cultic activities sponsored by a priesthood or the state. It does seem probable that Leviticus 16 and Num. 5:11–31 reflect a period dating from the monarchy or later when various Southern rulers and their priests attempt to centralize worship at the one sanctioned shrine in Jerusalem.

Num. 5:11–31 and Judg. 11:29–40, moreover, present two situations arising within the context of the same male-dominated view of female sexuality. The woman's reproductive capacity belongs to men and will be handed from father to husband under appropriate circumstances and at the appropriate time. Judg. 11:29–40, however, recognizes that the woman is an offering of sorts—a sacrifice, or, stated more positively, a most precious gift from one male to another—and allows the woman to prepare herself for this mediating role.

SUGGESTED READINGS

For a more detailed discussion of Exodus 12, see chapter 3 of Niditch's *Folklore and the Hebrew Bible* (1993a).

For helpful commentaries on Leviticus and Numbers that discuss priestly dimensions of Israelite ritual, see Milgrom and Levine. See Anderson for a useful monograph on ritual in Leviticus. For a study of women in Israelite law and ritual, see the essays by Bird.

On the interpretation of multivocalic symbols, see the methodology applied by Turner in *The Ritual Process* (1969). For a classic anthropological treatment of concepts of "clean" and "unclean" in traditional cultures, see Douglas's *Purity and Danger* (1966).

For a detailed study of Judg. 11:29–40 that explores the ritual of maturation implied by the narrative, see P. Day's essay "From the Child Is Born the Woman: The Story of Jephthah's Daughter."

Conclusion

After completing a course in Israelite religion, my students and I review what we have learned and prepare a list of themes that have emerged from our studies. I offer the same challenge to the reader of this book.

I hope you are able not only to identify with the ancient Israelites but also to distance yourself from your own tradition's understanding of them. How are the Israelites' problems still our problems? How do their lives and ours differ significantly? I hope you have come to appreciate the complexity of our source material, the challenges we face in interpreting biblical and extrabiblical sources, and the variety of Israelite culture itself.

In chapter 1, I outlined three major periods in Israelite history. First comes the pre-monarchic period (pre-tenth century B.C.E.), characterized by decentralized, small, agrarian, kinship-based communities. This period includes Israel's foundation in the frontier highlands.

Next come the northern and southern monarchies, in which urbanized capitals and some outlying fortified cities arise with distinctive architectural features. During this period (tenth–sixth centuries B.C.E.), national leadership comes to be held by a monarch surrounded by an elite or aristocratic class; attempts are made by such rulers to control the cult as well through priesthoods owing loyalty to them. There is an increase in the use of the technology of reading and writing, but the use of written words is framed by an oral aesthetic and an orally based mentality. The agrarian lifestyle, moreover, continues for the vast majority of Israelites, while kinship ties remain important markers of group and individual identity.

Lastly comes the post-monarchic period, following the Babylonian conquest of the southern Davidic kingdom, the destruction of the great temple built by Solomon in Jerusalem, and the exile of the elite to Babylon. The northern kingdom had already lost its independence in the Assyrian conquest of 722/1 B.C.E. The consensus of scholars maintains that conquest of the southern kingdom and loss of political autonomy bring a considerable reduction in Israelite material wealth, with a consequent shrinkage of major population centers. Yet it is at this time that much of the ancient Israelite library is collected, composed, or written down. It is during this period that the religion of ancient Israel makes a transition to early Judaism.

Certain pan-Israelite conditions and beliefs emerge from biblical and extrabiblical evidence: the importance of agriculture to the Israelite way of life; the importance of kinship ties through patrilineages; the orally based qualities of Israelite culture; love of Yahweh, who is world creator, rescuer–warrior, and Israel's lord in a covenantal relationship; the importance of ongoing mediation and communication between God and Israel expressed in various experiential genres, actualized in various forms of Israelite ritual and myth, and made possible by adherence to ethical demands believed to originate from God himself. Blood sacrifice remains an important medium of mediation throughout the tradition.

Within these contours are various competing and contrasting voices. The materials explored in this book suggest that some writers viewed God as more transcendent than others. Some practiced rituals to propitiate the dead and to secure fertility in the land, whereas others considered such practices non-Yahwistic. Some may have believed that Yahweh had a female consort, while others sublimated the notion through the figure of Wisdom or rejected it altogether. Kings, prophets, and priests serve to link Israel with the deity in much of the literature, but an equally strong thread in the tradition points to the role of ordinary Israelites in forging and maintaining their relationship with God.

Perhaps the most difficult problem faced by students of Israelite religion is the dating of biblical literature. Biblical texts are guides to the worldview of at least some Israelites, but the social and intellectual history of Israel spans almost a thousand years, and it is far from certain exactly where in that spectrum all of the texts originate. Materials collected in the Hebrew Bible had certainly become meaningful to members of the Israelite community, who finally combined and preserved them. This pan-Israelite library, however, preserves and accommodates the tensions and differences in worldview that contribute to ancient Israelite religion.

Some scholars in my field believe it impossible to match up any portion of the biblical corpus with voices and worldviews that predate the exile. Others ignore the question of context altogether and instead read the Bible ahistorically as a work of literature in which they seek the messages that biblical texts extend to them as modern readers.

I have ventured, albeit tentatively, to match texts with social contexts. It is important to note that an ancient song such as Exodus 15, provably early according to orthographic and metric considerations, would be interpreted by believing communities to apply to later periods as well. Narratives such as the story of Eden and law codes such as the Ten Commandments might have held great meaning in premonarchic times, remaining formative and self-defining throughout the history of Israelite religion. I have traced some of the recurring clusters of content that hold the tradition together, such as the covenant form, the annunciation, and the victory–enthronement pattern. Employed with nuances and variations, these forms express the worldviews of Israelites of various persuasions and periods. Such recurring forms, in fact, serve as templates of variations in Israelite worldview at a given time and through time as we ask how a common literary pattern has been individualized and contextualized by a particular author in a particular life setting. I have also looked behind the dominant voices in the Hebrew Bible to explore the lost, hidden, or repressed points of view in the tradition. Interest in Israelite attitudes toward the realm of the dead and in women's religious lives have been important threads in my work.

This book offers only a first taste of the rich and various religious traditions of ancient Israel and is meant to serve as an invitation to further study.

TIMELINE

	Key Dates/Events	Characters	Tenor of the Times
Pre-monarchic Period **13th–11th centuries** BCE			Decentralized government: Israelite village culture predominates; possible role of chieftains; prevalence of pillared houses in cluster arrangements; importance of kinship ties; oral culture.
1230 BCE	Mention of Israel in Merneptah Stele		
The Monarchies **10th–6th centuries** BCE			While village life, kinship bonds, and oral tradition remain important for maintenance and understanding of Israelite culture, there are some urban centers in north and south, centralized militaries, many more extant examples of writing, aristocracies, building projects funded by tolls and taxes, and slave labor.
10th century BCE	United Monarchy; building of Temple in Jerusalem	David; Solomon	
922 BCE	Split between Northern and Southern Kingdom (Israel and Judah)		
8th century BCE		Omri, Ahab, Jezebel (Northern dynasty) Elijah, Elisha, prophets in Israel	
722/1 BCE	Fall of Samaria (Israel) to Assyrians	Classical prophet/poets, Isaiah and Micah in Judah and Amos and Hosea in Israel	
701 BCE	Assyrian conquest of the Judean fortress-city, Lachish		

Date	Event	Figure / Notes
640–609 BCE	Reign of Josiah, a Southern reforming king. Some would date composition of Deut-2 Kings to this period	Jeremiah, the prophet whose career spans late 7th century to the time of the exile
Post-monarchic Period 6th century BCE on		Most scholars regard this period as one of hardship with reduced population centers, loss of political autonomy, and economic deprivation, a time of transformation and restructuring for ancient Israel, but a time of great literary creativity, perhaps the time when much of the Israelite literary traditions as we recognize them in the Hebrew Bible are composed or preserved.
597 BCE	1st Babylonian exile	Ezekiel, the priest/prophet whose career continues into the major period of exile
587/6 BCE	Fall of Jerusalem, 2nd exile	
538 BCE	Edict by Persian Cyrus allowing Jews to return and rebuild temple	2 Isaiah prophet/poet of Isaiah 40–55
520–515 BCE	Rebuilding of temple in Jerusalem	Haggai and Zechariah, pro-temple prophets
5th century BCE	Ezra "the scribe" and Nehemiah, governor of Judea, each of whom comes to Jerusalem under Persian auspices to strengthen and reconstruct Jewish polity in accordance with particular religious ideals and Persian policy.	

APPENDIX

Questions for Further Study

Chapter 1

1. Having read the works by Smart, Berger, or Geertz, try to apply their insights to a religious tradition with which you are familiar. Some scholars suggest that there is an American secular religion with its own symbol systems, sacred calendar, etc. What do you think?

2. Are you surprised by the archaeologists' rendition of Israelite history? What surprises you most and why?

3. Which theories of biblical composition do you find most convincing and why?

4. Try to imagine what life was like for men and women farmers in pre-monarchic times. Describe your daily existence as a man or woman living in Jerusalem during the monarchy if your livelihood were closely tied to the monarchy?

5. Can you imagine what life would be like in an oral–traditional culture? Discuss.

Chapter 2

Read and discuss some "experiential scenes" in the Hebrew Bible not explored in chapter 2. The following are excellent examples.

1. Read Josh. 5:13–15, where the biblical hero encounters the commander of God's divine armies before the battle of Jericho. This scene is a common ancient Near Eastern topos wherein the deity appears, sword outstretched, to a leader before battle. How does this scene compare with others in the Hebrew Bible? Discuss this example of the experiential in its biblical setting.

2. Read Judg. 6:11–24. How does this theophany compare with the others? Is a conventionalized pattern employed? If so, with what nuances? What is the function of the fire motif?

3. Read 1 Kings 18, the scene in which the prophets of Baal and Elijah and his followers compete, seeking to prove their deity's capacity to manifest himself, to be experienced. How does Yahweh's power emerge? What is the implicit worldview that frames this passage?

4. Explore the two scenes that are said to give rise to the proverb "Is Saul, too, among the prophets?" (1 Sam. 10:9–13 and 19:20–24). Describe the prophetic frenzy. What is the implicit view of the experiential in these passages? How does the scene in 1 Sam. 19 differ from the one in 1 Sam. 10 in terms of the attitudes toward Saul and the quality of his experience.

5. An interesting trajectory in the category of the experiential is formed by the symbolic visions in Amos 7:7–9; 8:1–3, Jer. 1:11–12, 13–19; Jeremiah 24, Zechariah 1–6, and Dan 7–8. Explore this set of passages. What is the overriding literary form and how do its various uses differ, thereby revealing differences in Israelite worldview? Do certain thematic patterns and developments emerge? Discuss.

Chapter 3

Read Genesis 1–11 and answer the following questions:

1. If one defines creation not merely as the coming to be of the world but also as the ordering of what is there, how many creation accounts are there in Genesis 1–11? What are their various structures and themes? Do certain patterns emerge and recur? Discuss.

2. Compare some of the creation tales in Genesis 1–11 with the stories of victory–enthronement presented in this chapter. What continuities or contrasts emerge? What are some of the implications of your findings for understanding Israelite worldview?

3. Why do you think that a pervasive ancient Near Eastern creation pattern has a violent war at its center? Discuss.

4. Do Israelite views of origins tally with views of death to construct certain consistent worldviews? Discuss.

5. How do Israelite notions of death and customs concerning the dead compare and contrast with your own? What surprised you, if anything, about this aspect of Israelite worldview?

Chapter 4

1. The prophetic corpus is rich in examples of the lawsuit. Read Amos 5, Hosea 2, and Hosea 4 and discuss how the prophet has employed this tradi-

tional form, rooted in notions of covenant, to speak to Israelites in a specific setting.

2. Some scholars believe that all the covenants in the Hebrew Bible are implicitly conditional. Do you agree? Discuss.

3. What are sources of chaos in modern Western culture? What about your own "folk" group?

4. Do we symbolically attempt to impose some sense of order on the inherently chaotic nature of our existence? How?

5. What most surprised you in about legal codes?

6. What views of women are revealed in the legal texts?

7. Define "liberal" versus "conservative" as these terms might pertain to Israelite law. Discuss in terms of economic, political, and family ethics.

8. Do the materials we have explored describe community in different ways? Contrast and compare.

9. What would it be like to live in the Deuteronomic ideal world? Discuss.

10. Do the codes reveal surprising attitudes toward human sexuality? Discuss.

Chapter 5

1. Discuss some ritual patterns in your own culture. Do certain recurring symbols emerge? Do modern societies have their own rituals or feel the need for ritual? Discuss.

2. Are you at all able to identify with Israelites who practice sacrificial rituals. Why or why not?

3. How does your study of Israelite ritual tally with what you have learned about other aspects of Israelite religion?

4. How have celebrations of Passover and Yom Kippur been transformed in classical and modern Judaism?

5. Concerning the troubling material on women in Numbers 5 and Judges 11, are attitudes in these texts current today? Have we been in part shaped by such biblical texts? For a special topic, explore the transformation of Num. 5:11–31 in classical Judaism by studying Mishnah Soṭah.

6. Read Deut. 21:1–9 carefully. It presents the case of an unsolved murder. No witnesses are available. Why is the matter troubling and disruptive and how is it dealt with ritually? Discuss the ritual pattern and its symbols in detail. Draw appropriate comparisons with material presented in this chapter. What does this ritual suggest about an author's worldview?

7. Note the way in which the description of the Passover in Exodus 12 compares and contrasts with more centralized versions in Deuteronomy and 1–2 Chronicles. What do these differences suggest about some of the various threads in Israelite worldview?

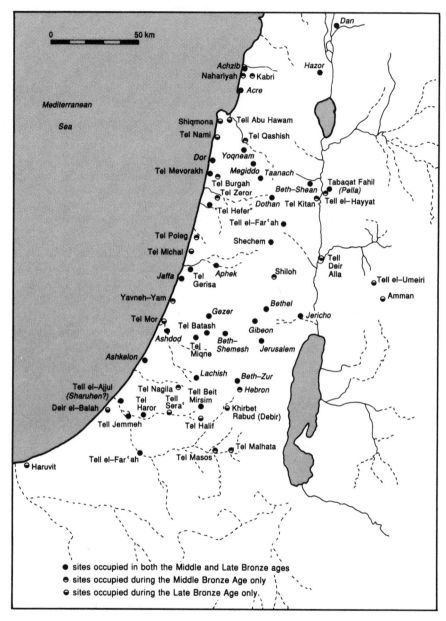

Map 1. Map of Middle Bronze II and Late Bronze Age Excavated Sites. Place names in *italics* are ancient names; plate names in roman letters are modern names. (*Maps 1–3 drawn by Rahel Solar, are provided courtesy of Professor Amihai Mazar.*)

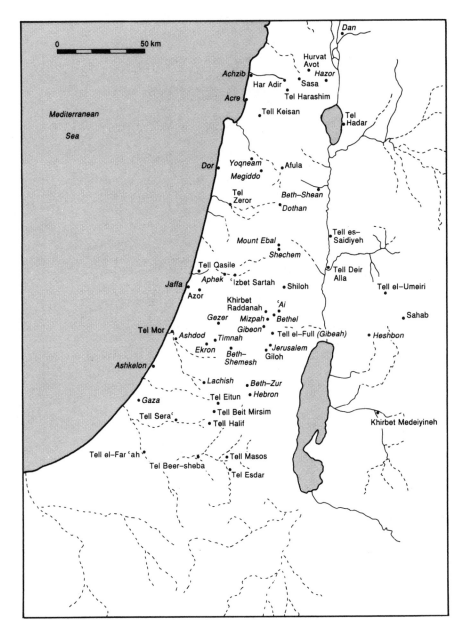

Map 2. Map of Iron Age I Sites. Ancient names are in italics; modern names are in roman.

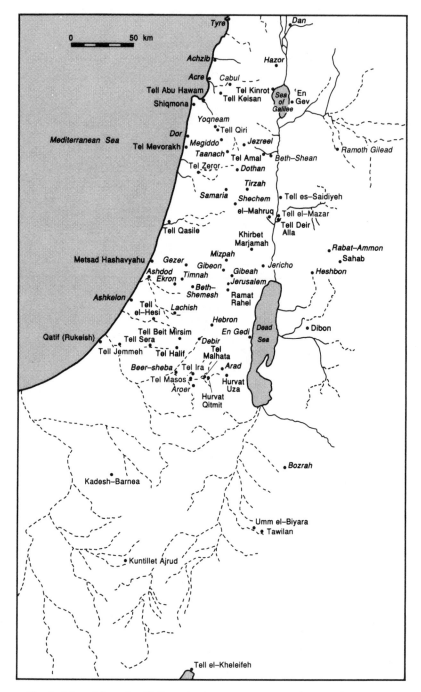

Map 3. Map of Iron Age II Sites. Ancient names are in italics, modern names in roman.

BIBLIOGRAPHY

Abbreviations

ABD	*Anchor Bible Dictionary.* 6 vols. Garden City, N.Y.: Doubleday, 1992
ANET	*Ancient Near Eastern Texts,* ed. James B. Pritchard. Princeton: Princeton University Press, 1969
BA	*Biblical Archaeologist*
BAR	*Biblical Archaeology Review*
BASOR	*Bulletin of the American Schools of Oriental Research*
BDB	F. Brown, S. R. Driver, and C. A. Briggs, *A Hebrew and English Lexicon of the Old Testament.* Oxford: Clarendon Press, 1968
BZAW	Beihefte zur *Zeitschrift für die alttestamentliche Wissenschaft*
CBQMS	Catholic Biblical Quarterly Monograph Series. Washington, D.C.: Catholic Biblical Association of America
HAR	*Hebrew Annual Review*
HSM	Harvard Semitic Monographs
HTR	*Harvard Theological Review*
HUCA	*Hebrew Union College Annual*
NRSV	New Revised Standard Version of the Bible
JBL	*Journal of Biblical Literature*
JSOT	*Journal for the Study the Old Testament*
SBLDS	SBL Dissertation Series

Ackerman, Susan. 1992. *Under Every Green Tree. Popular Religion in Sixth-Century Judah.* HSM 46. Atlanta: Scholars Press.

———. 1993. "The Queen Mother and the Cult in Ancient Israel." *JBL* 112: 385–401.

Alter, Robert. 1981. *The Art of Biblical Narrative.* New York: Basic Books.

Anderson, Gary A. 1987. *Sacrifices and Offerings in Ancient Israel: Studies in Their Social and Political Importance*. Atlanta: Scholars Press.

Avigad, N. 1987. "The Contribution of Hebrew Seals to an Understanding of Israelite Religion and Society." In *Ancient Israelite Religion*, ed. Patrick D. Miller et al. Pp. 145–208.

Barkay, Gabriel 1992. "The Iron Age II–III." In *The Archaeology of Ancient Israel*, ed. Ben-Tor. Pp. 302–73.

Ben-Tor, Amnon, ed. 1992. *The Archaeology of Ancient Israel*. New Haven: Yale University Press.

Berger, Peter. 1967. *The Sacred Canopy: Elements of a Sociological Theory of Religion*. Garden City, N.Y.: Doubleday.

Biran, Avraham. 1985. *Biblical Archaeology Today*. Proceedings of the International Congress on Biblical Archaeology Jerusalem. April. Jerusalem: Israel Exploration Society.

Bird, Phyllis. 1974. "Images of Women in the Old Testament." In *Religion and Sexism*, ed. Rosemary Radford Ruether. Pp. 41–88. New York: Simon and Schuster.

———. 1987. "The Place of Women in the Israelite Cultus." In *Ancient Israelite Religion*, ed. P. D. Miller et al. Pp. 397–420.

Bloch-Smith, Elizabeth. 1992. "The Cult of the Dead in Judah: Interpreting the Material Remains." *JBL* 111:213–24.

Brichto, Herbert Chanan. 1973. "Kin, Cult, Land, and Afterlife: A Biblical Complex." *HUCA* 44:1–54.

Bright, John. 1981. *A History of Israel*. 3rd ed. Philadelphia: Westminster Press.

Brown, Kay. 1978. *Beauty and the Beast*. New York: Derrydale.

Carmichael, Callum 1974. *The Laws of Deuteronomy*. Ithaca, N.Y.: Cornell University Press.

———. 1979. *Women, Law, and the Genesis Traditions*. Ithaca, N.Y.: Cornell University Press.

———. 1992. *The Origins of Biblical Law: The Decalogues and the Book of the Covenant*. Ithaca, N.Y.: Cornell University Press.

Carter, Charles Edward. 1992. "A Social and Demographic Study of Post-Exilic Judah." Ph.D. diss., Duke University.

Clifford, Richard J. 1994. *Creation Accounts in the Ancient Near East and the Bible*. CBQMS 26. Washington, D.C.: Catholic Biblical Association.

Collins, John J. 1989. *The Apocalyptic Imagination*. New York: Crossroad.

Cook, Stephen L. 1995. *Prophecy and Apocalypticism: The Post-Exilic Social Setting*. Minneapolis: Fortress Press.

Coogan, Michael D. 1987. "Canaanite Origins and Lineage: Reflections on the Religion of Ancient Israel." In *Ancient Israelite Religion*, ed. P. Miller et al. Pp. 115–24.

Coote, Robert B. 1991. *In Defense of Revolution: The Elohist History.* Minneapolis: Augsburg/Fortress Press.

Coote, Robert B., and David Robert Ord. 1989. *The Bible's First History.* Philadelphia: Fortress Press.

Cross, Frank Moore. 1973. *Canaanite Myth and Hebrew Epic.* Cambridge, Mass.: Harvard University Press.

———. 1974. "Prose and Poetry in the Mythic and Epic Texts from Ugarit." *HTR* 61:1–15.

Cross, Frank Moore, and David Noel Freedman. 1975. *Studies in Ancient Yahwistic Poetry.* SBLDS 21. Missoula, Mont.: Scholars Press.

Day, John. 1989. *Molech: A God of Human Sacrifice in Old Testament.* University of Cambridge Oriental Publications 41. Cambridge: Cambridge University Press.

Day, Peggy L. 1989a. "From the Child Is Born the Woman: The Story of Jephthah's Daughter." In *Gender and Difference in Ancient Israel*, ed. P. Day. Pp. 58–74.

———, ed. 1989b. *Gender and Difference in Ancient Israel.* Minneapolis: Fortress Press.

Doty, William. 1986. *Mythography. The Study of Myths and Rituals.* University, Al.: Univerity of Alabama Press.

Douglas, Mary. 1966. *Purity and Danger: An Analysis of Concepts of Pollution and Taboo.* New York: Praeger.

Dundes, Alan. 1988. "The Flood as Male Myth of Creation." In *The Flood Myth*, ed. Alan Dundes. Pp. 167–82. Berkeley: University of California Press.

Eilberg-Schwartz, Howard 1994. *God's Phallus.* Boston: Beacon.

———. 1990. *The Savage in Judaism: An Anthropology of Israelite Religion and Ancient Judaism.* Bloomington: Indiana University Press.

Eliade, Mircea. 1964. *Shamanism: Archaic Techniques of Ecstasy.* Bollingen Ser. 76. Princeton, N.J.: Princeton University Press.

———. 1965. *The Myth of the Eternal Return.* Bollingen Series 46. Princeton, N.J.: Princeton University Press.

Exum, J. Cheryl. 1980. "Promise and Fulfillment: Narrative Art in Judges 13." *JBL* 99:39–59.

Feeley-Harnik, Gillian. 1990. "Naomi and Ruth: Building Up the House of David." In *Text and Tradition*, ed. Niditch. Pp. 163–84.

Finkelstein, Israel. 1985. "Response." In *Biblical Archaeology Today*, ed. A. Biran, Pp. 80–83.

Friedman, Richard E. 1987. *Who Wrote the Bible?* Englewood Cliffs, N.J.: Prentice-Hall.

Frazer, Sir James G. 1918. *Folklore in the Old Testament.* 3 vols. London: MacMillan.

Gaster, Theodore. 1969. *Myth, Legend, and Custom in the Old Testament: A Comparative Study with Chapters from Sir James G. Frazer's "Folklore in the Old Testament."* 2 vols. Gloucester, Mass.: Peter Smith.

Geertz, Clifford. 1973. *The Interpretation of Cultures: Selected Essays.* New York: Basic Books.

Goody, Jack, ed. 1968. *Literacy in Traditional Societies.* Cambridge: Cambridge University Press.

Gottwald, Norman. 1964. " 'Holy War' in Deuteronomy: Analysis and Critique." *Review and Exposition* 61:297–310.

Greenstein, Edward L. 1984. "Biblical Law." In *Back to the Sources,* ed. Holtz. Pp. 83–103.

Gunn, David M., and Dana Fewell. 1993. *Narrative in the Hebrew Bible.* Oxford: Oxford University Press.

Hackett, Jo Ann. 1987. "Religious Traditions in Israelite Transjordan." In *Ancient Israelite Religion,* ed. P. D. Miller et al. Pp. 125–36.

Hanson, Paul D. 1975. *The Dawn of Apocalyptic.* Philadelphia: Fortress Press.

Heidel, Alexander. 1951. *The Babylonian Genesis.* Chicago: University of Chicago Press.

Heider, George C. 1985. *The Cult of Molek: A Reassessment.* Sheffield, Eng.: JSOT Press.

Hendel, Ronald S. 1987. *The Epic of the Patriarch: The Jacob Cycle and the Narrative Traditions of Canaan and Israel.* HSM 42. Atlanta: Scholars Press.

Hibbitts, Bernard J. 1992. " 'Coming to Our Senses': Communication and Legal Expression in Performance Cultures." *Emory Law Journal* 41:873–960.

Hillers, Delbert R. 1969. *Covenant: The History of a Biblical Idea.* Baltimore: The Johns Hopkins University Press.

Hogland, Kenneth G. 1992. *Achaemenid Imperial Administration in Syria-Palestine and the Missions of Ezra and Nehemiah.* SBLDS 125. Atlanta: Scholars Press.

Holladay, John S., Jr. 1987. "Religion in Israel and Judah Under the Monarchy: An Explicitly Archaeological Approach," In *Ancient Israelite Religion,* ed. P. D. Miller et al. Pp. 249–99.

———. 1994. "The Kingdoms of Israel and Judah: Political and Economic Centralization in the Iron II a–b (ca. 1000–750 B.C.E.)." Unpublished longer draft of a chapter in *The Archaeology of Society in the Holy Land,* ed. Thomas E. Levy. London: Pintner.

———. 1992. "House, Israelite." ABD 3:308–20.

Holtz, Barry W. 1984. *Back to the Sources: Reading the Classic Jewish Texts.* New York: Summit Books.

Hurwitz, Avi. 1974. "The Date of the Prose-Tale of Job Linguistically Reconsidered." *HTR* 67:17–34.

Hyatt, J. P. 1971. *Commentary on Exodus: The New Century Bible.* London: Olpihants.

Irvin, Dorothy. 1977. "The Joseph and Moses Stories as Narrative in the Light of Ancient Near Eastern Narrative." In *Israelite and Judaean History*, ed. J. H. Hayes and J. M. Miller. Pp. 180–209. Philadelphia: Westminster Press.

———. 1978. *Mytharion: The Comparison of Tales from the Old Testament and the Ancient Near East.* Veroffentlichungen zum Kultur und Geschichte des Alten Testaments 32. Neukirchen-Vluyn: Neukirchener Verlag.

Jacobsen, Thorkild. 1968. "Mesopotamia: The Cosmos as a State." In *Before Philosophy*, by H. and H. A. Frankfort, John A. Wilson, and Thorkild Jacobsen. Pp. 137–99. Baltimore, Md.: Penguin Books.

Knight, Douglas A. 1983. "Wellhausen and the Interpretation of Israel's Literature." In *Julius Wellhausen and His Prolegomena to the History of Israel*, ed. Douglas A. Knight. Pp. 21–36. Semeia Studies 25. Chico, Ca.: Scholars Press.

Levenson, Jon. 1993. *The Death and Resurrection of the Beloved Son. The Transformation of Child Sacrifice in Judaism and Christianity.* New Haven: Yale University Press.

Levine, Baruch A. 1989. *Leviticus: The Traditional Hebrew Text with the New JPS Translation. Commentary by Baruch A. Levine.* Philadelphia: Jewish Publication Society.

Lewis, Theodore J. 1987. "Death Cult Imagery in Isaiah 57." *HAR* 11:267–84.

———. 1989. *Cults of the Dead in Ancient Israel and Ugarit.* HSM 39. Atlanta: Scholars Press.

Little, David, and Sumner B. Twiss. 1978. *Comparative Religious Ethics.* San Francisco: Harper and Row.

McCarter, P. Kyle. 1987. "Aspects of the Religion of the Israelite Monarchy: Biblical and Epigraphic Data." In *Ancient Israelite Religion*, ed. P. D. Miller, et al. Pp. 137–55.

Mazar, Amihai. 1992. *Archaeology of the Land of Israel.* New York: Doubleday.

Mendenhall, George E. 1954. "Law and Covenant in Israel and the Ancient Near East." *BA* 17:49–76.

Meyers, Carol. 1988. *Discovering Eve: Ancient Israelite Women in Context.* New York: Oxford University Press.

———. forthcoming A. "The Family in Early Israel." In *The Family in Ancient Israel and Early Judaism*, ed. Purdue.

———. forthcoming B. "Kinship and Kingship: The Early Monarchy." Chap. 6 of *The Oxford History of the Biblical World*, ed. Coogan.

Milgrom, Jacob. 1990. *Numbers: The Traditional Hebrew Text with the New JPS Translation. Commentary by Jacob Milgrom.* Philadelphia: Jewish Publication Society.

———. 1991. *Leviticus: A New Translation with Introduction and Commentary.* New York: Doubleday.

Miller, Geoffrey. 1993. "Contracts of Genesis 22." *Journal of Legal Studies* 22: 15–45.

———. 1995. "J as a Constitutionalist: A Political Interpretation of Exodus 17:8–16 and Related Texts." *Chicago-Kent Law Review* 70:1829–1847.

Miller, Patrick D.; Paul D. Hanson; and S. Dean McBride, eds. 1987. *Ancient Israelite Religion: Essays in Honor of Frank Moore Cross.* Philadelphia: Fortress Press.

Niditch, Susan. 1980a. *The Symbolic Vision in Biblical Tradition.* HSM 30. Chico, Ca.: Scholars Press.

———. 1980b. "The Visionary." In *Ideal Figures in Ancient Judaism*, eds. George W. E. Nickelsburg and John J. Collins. Pp. 153–79. Septuagint and Cognate Studies 12. Chico, Ca.: Scholars Press.

———. 1985. *Chaos to Cosmos. Studies in Biblical Patterns of Creation.* Chico, Ca: Scholars Press.

———. 1987. *Underdogs and Tricksters: A Prelude to Biblical Folklore.* San Francisco: Harper and Row.

———. 1992. "Genesis." In *The Women's Bible Commentary*, ed. Carol A. Newsom and Sharon H. Ringe. Pp. 10–25. Louisville, Ky.: Westminster/ John Knox Press.

———. 1993a. *Folklore and the Hebrew Bible.* Minneapolis: Fortress Press.

———. 1993b. *War in the Hebrew Bible: A Study in the Ethics of Violence.* New York: Oxford University Press.

———. ed. 1990. *Text and Tradition. The Hebrew Bible and Folklore.* Semeia Studies. Atlanta: Scholars Press.

Nielsen, Eduard. 1961. *Oral Tradition: A Modern Problem in Old Testament Introduction.* London: SCM.

Olyan, Saul. 1988. *Ashera and the Cult of Yahweh in Israel.* Atlanta: Scholars Press.

Oppenheim, A. Leo. 1964. *Ancient Mesopotamia.* Chicago: University of Chicago Press.

Otto, Rudolf. 1928. *The Idea of the Holy.* London: Oxford University Press.

Pedersen, Johannes. 1926/1940. *Israel: Its Life and Culture.* Vols. 1–2/3–4. London: Oxford University Press.

Polzin, Robert. 1980. *Moses and the Deuteronomist: A Literary Study of the Deuteronomic History.* Part I. *Deuteronomy, Joshua, Judges.* New York: Seabury Press.

Pressler, Carolyn. 1993. *The View of Women Found in the Deuteronomic Family Laws.* BZAW 216. Berlin and New York: de Gruyter.

Pritchard, James A. 1969. *Ancient Near Eastern Texts.* Princeton, N.J.: Princeton University Press.

Rad, Gerhard von. 1976 [1953]. "The Joseph Narrative and Ancient Wisdom." In *Studies in Ancient Israelite Wisdom*, ed. James L. Crenshaw. Pp. 439–47. New York: KTAV.

Rendtorff, R. 1986. *The Old Testament: An Introduction*. Trans. John Bowden. Philadelphia: Fortress Press.

Rose, Martin 1981. *Deuteronomist und Jahwist: Untersuchungen zu den Berührungspunkten beiden Literarwerke*. Zurich: Theologischer Verlag.

Schmidt, Brian B. 1995. *Israel's Beneficent Dead: Ancestor Cult and Necromancy in Israelite Religion and Tradition*. Tübingen: J. C. B. Mohr.

Smart, Ninian. 1960. *World Religions: A Dialogue*. Baltimore: Penguin Books.
———. 1969. *The Religious Experience of Mankind*. New York: Scribner.
———. 1983. *Worldviews: Cross-Cultural Explorations of Human Beliefs*. New York: Scribner.

Smelik, Klaas A. D. 1991. *Writings from Ancient Israel*. Louisville, Ky: Westminster/John Knox Press.

Smith, Mark. 1990. *The Early History of God: Yahweh and Other Deities in Ancient Israel*. New York: Harper-Collins.

Speiser, E. A. 1964. *Genesis*. Anchor Bible 1. Garden City, N.Y.: Doubleday.

Sproul, Barbara C. 1979. *Primal Myths: Creating the World*. San Francisco: Harper and Row.

Stager, Lawrence E. 1985. "The Archaeology of the Family in Ancient Israel." *BASOR* 260:1–35.
———. 1989. "The Song of Deborah: Why Some Tribes Answered the Call and Others Did Not." *BAR* 15:50–64.

Stern, Ephraim. 1982. *Material Culture of the Land of the Bible in the Persian Period, 538–332 B.C.* Warminster, England: Aris and Phillips.

Stulman, Lewis. 1990. "Encroachment in Deuteronomy: An Analysis of the Social World of the D Code." *JBL* 109:613–32.

Thompson, Thomas. 1992. *Early History of the Israelite People: From the Written and Archaeological Sources*. Leiden: Brill.

Tigay, Jeffrey H. 1987. "Israelite Religion: The Onomastic and Epigraphic Evidence." In *Ancient Israelite Religion*, ed. P. D. Miller. Pp. 157–94.

Turner, Victor. 1969. *The Ritual Process*. Ithaca, N.Y.: Cornell University Press.

Van Seters, John. 1977. *Abraham in History and Tradition*. New Haven: Yale University Press.
———. 1983. *In Search of History: Historiography in the Ancient World and the Origins of Biblical History*. New Haven: Yale University Press.
———. 1992. *Prologue to History: The Yahwist as Historian in Genesis*. Louisville, Ky.: Westminster/John Knox, Press.

Walls, Neal H. 1992. *The Goddess Anat in Ugaritic Myth*. SBLDS 135. Atlanta: Scholars Press.

Wellhausen, Julius. 1983. *Prolegomena to the History of Israel*. With a Preface by W. Robertson Smith. Edinburgh: Adam and Charles Black; rpt. New York: Meridian Books, 1957. (Trans. of *Geschichte Israels. In zwei Bänden. Erster Band*. Berlin: Reimer, 1878; 2nd ed. *Prolegomena zur Geschichte Israels*. Berlin: Reimer, 1883).

Wilson, Robert R. 1987. "Prophecy in Crisis: The Call of Ezekiel." In *Interpreting the Prophets*, Ed., James L. Mays and Paul J. Achtemeir. Pp. 157–69 Phildelphia: Fortress Press.

INDEX OF BIBLICAL CITATIONS

GENERAL INDEX